H

FALL BACK IN LOVE WITH YOUR BUSINESS

THE ENTREPRENEUR'S GUIDE TO
REDISCOVERING YOUR MOJO AND
ENJOYING EVERY DAY BY LIVING YOUR
DREAM

ADRIAN PECK

BETTER NEVER STOPS®

First published by PeckUK Limited 2019

First edition

ISBN 978-1-9163094-0-1 (paperback)

ISBN 978-1-9163094-1-8 (ebook)

Dedicated to:

My Mum & Dad – Who gave me the values and 'stock' that I treasure dearly.

My Family & Friends – Life has no meaning without sharing the love of Hannah, Haiden, my family and friends: you inspire me every day.

My Brothers – Roger, Ian and Patrick, you are and will always be my brothers.

My Wife & Best Friend: Suzanne, you are my life. I'm so proud of what we have achieved and excited about what lies ahead.

CONTENTS

FOREWORD

by Richard Jackson MBE

This book is like no other that I have read in the personal/business improvement field, and I've read quite a few in the past three-odd decades. Its scope is enormous; the number and the breadth of subjects covered, and the amount of detail and pragmatic, practical advice given is prodigious.

Aimed at entrepreneurs and business owners with companies whose turnover is around £1m or more, How to Fall Back in Love with your Business is a provocative title that immediately has the reader asking themselves the question of whether they have fallen out of love with their own company.

I decided, after a certain amount of self-reflection, that I hadn't fallen out of love with my company, Mancroft International, but that there were aspects of the business that I now found tiresome or frustrating, and I used not to feel that way thirty-five years ago when I founded the company.

My personal development programme, the Winning Edge, specialises in how important the appropriate mindset is to being successful in business and in life generally, and this book is an extremely important addition to the genre, as it comes at the subject in a different way and in a way that is pragmatic and completely practical.

There are chapters on Strategy, Empowerment, Control, CASH – an intriguing acronym – Efficiency, Scale, Making it Happen and The Entrepreneurs Guide to Having Fun and Living the Dream; an interesting and eclectic range of subjects and all highly relevant to running a successful company while enjoying the journey.

The most important feeling that you will have if you implement all that is recommended in this book is of control, and there is a direct link between feeling in control and being a better leader, manager, driver, parent, influencer, salesperson – need I go on?

Enjoy this book, it can change your life and have you Falling in Love with your Business again.

 **Richard Jackson MBE** is the Co-founder of The Winning Edge Programmes and Director of Mancroft International. Since 1984, Richard has presented 'The Winning Edge' programme to over 175,000 people throughout the World, consistently inspiring his audiences to greater performance and achievement. In the 2014 New Years' Honours list, Richard was awarded an MBE for services to Development and Corporate Training.

INTRODUCTION

The Entrepreneur's Journey

A few years ago you started your business, either on your own or with a business partner or partners. There's a high chance that you come from a technical background and are good at what you do.

In fact, you're so good you've decided "hell, I can do this, why am I working for this idiot? Why don't I set up my own company and 'sail my own boat'?" And you have. You started your own business with great plans and, for a number of years, it has grown well, based on your sheer determination, hard work and passion.

In time you have managed to get it over the £1m turnover 'mountain' and you've taken on employees. You may not realise it but, even by employing more than three people, you are in the top 20% of UK businesses and, if you have more than nine employees, you are in the top 4%. In fact, if you earn more than £63,000 per year (ONS 2018), you are in the top 3% of earners in the UK, so well done for getting this far.

So what's next?

And this is where it's most likely you've got stuck. The growth of your business has now slowed down, has plateaued or dropped back. Since you started the business has changed considerably, and you've changed with it. I've noticed a few significant things happening as people get older:

1. You become less tolerant of people and poor service.

2. You get more cynical.

3. You start to really value your time.

This last one is the most significant when it comes to your business. When you started out you had a dream about how your life was going to pan out, all the things you were going to do. But the greatest challenge to you now is TIME. Where does it go to? You start every week with great gusto, determined you're going to smash that to-do list; you're going to get on with doing the things you want and love to do. Monday comes, you drive into work with your master plan and…all manner of shit happens and, before you know it, BAM! It's Friday again.

Everyone tells you "You should be working on your business and not in it." Yeah right, how are you going to do that, and who's going to get done what you normally get done?

As the weeks and months roll by you are more worn down and frustrated. Yes, there are some highs but it's not what you really want, and you know you can achieve so much more. You start to look overly forward to weekends and holidays and, before long, you've become an employee. You have lost sight of the reason you started the business, and in the words of Bob Geldof, you "Don't like Mondays". Life is starting to feel a bit like

Groundhog Day: every week is filled with unwanted noise and, before you know it, it's the weekend again. You have started to become bored, easily distracted, disinterested and have lost your mojo.

Managing people is a nightmare. Your business has grown, and so has the number of staff, but the people issues have multiplied well beyond the growth curve. Managing people has become stressful and unrewarding. No-one except you seems to get the business, or seems to care about it, or share the same goals.

Where has all the money gone? Your turnover has grown, you're employing more people, you have more customers and you're working harder than ever. But, at the end of each year, the accountant reports lower profits and your earnings don't increase. You want to start living your life and you deserve more for all the hard work you have put in, and the risks you have taken.

If you haven't already, or you have, but not quite realised that you have, you will start to fall out of love with your business. You have started to fall out of love with your business. How do you know?

- You've lost the passion and drive you once felt.

- You're bored and easily distracted.

- You've stopped thinking about the future.

- You're difficult to live with, more aggressive, angry or distant.

- You procrastinate more or find it hard to make important decisions.

- You try to fill your weekends with really exciting stuff to make up for the weekdays.

- You blame the industry, the economy, your competitors or anyone else.

- You're not as proud as you once were about what you've achieved.

- You're frustrated and stressed.

But there's something else lurking deep inside…

The Fear of Failure

Deep down you believe you know a lot about what you need to do to take your business forward. You've also possibly read some books, attended the odd seminar and talked to others about it. So what's stopping you?

Without knowing it you've also developed a fear of failure. You're worried that you have built your business this far and, if you try to change it, it could all come tumbling down and you will lose everything.

So, the best thing to do is to bury your head in the sand and 'pretend/hope/kid yourself' something magical will happen, and it will change.

How can I fall back in love with my business?

You are not alone.

All your feelings, challenges and fears are a normal part of the Entrepreneur's Journey and shared across most £1m-plus growing businesses. Of course, nobody talks about it. Most of these companies are run by men over 40 years old, and hell, we're never going to talk about our feelings to each other. If you ask "How's your business going?" the answer will be "Oh, we're so busy…" But most aren't doing that well so don't be fooled into thinking you're alone and the only one in the situation.

Your strength now is to recognise the traits and signs mentioned above and do something about it.

That's why I've written this book, to give you a safe place to go and find a proven system to get your love for your business back on track. By reading and implementing the principles that I'm going to share with you in this book, your business will be easier and more enjoyable to manage. Through focus, better utilisation of your team, and by doing the things you enjoy, you'll achieve the aspirational results you desire and fall back in love with your business. Real results drive wealth and, in turn, you will start to live the dream that your hard work deserves.

It's time to stop procrastinating. One of my clients, and now a good friend, Adrian Lewis, has a great saying (he's from Yorkshire so it's even better in his accent):

"Only shit happens, everything else you have to make happen."

The Seven Steps to SECCESS®

Through the book, I'm going to show you the seven steps to SECCESS®. Yes I know SECCESS is spelt incorrectly, but that's for two very good reasons:

1. It stands for Strategy, Empowerment, Control, CASH, Efficiency, Separate & Scale. I could have used Unity instead of Empowerment but it just didn't convey the same importance of a team.

2. I'm dyslexic, so it looks perfectly OK to me…

Since 2011 I've met and worked with hundreds of entrepreneurs like you, experiencing the same challenges, pains and frustrations. I've recognised that it doesn't matter what industry you're in, or what type of business you run, you all experience the same challenges. So, I've developed this seven-step system that will work for every entrepreneur running a £1m-plus turnover company.

In each chapter I'll take you through each step and the principle that it's based on:

Strategy – Enjoy the journey, it's more important than the destination

Empowerment – You'll only achieve exceptional results through effective teamwork

Control Panel – Know what you want, measure, assess and drive performance

Cash – Your primary goal must focus on generating real cash

Efficiency – Get more for less through constant review and utilisation of technology

Separate – Stand out by adding value to increase the demand and margins

Scale – Always be selling

With every step there are supporting templates, charts, examples and additional content to be found on our website: www.betterneverstops.global/tools. These are all free to download and use to implement the seven steps into your business.

One last thing, when I talk about products I'm referring to any product or service you sell.

Let's get started...

STRATEGY

"Would you tell me, please, which way I ought to go from here?"

"That depends a good deal on where you want to get to."

"I don't much care where –"

"Then it doesn't matter which way you go."

— Lewis Carroll, Alice in Wonderland

I'm sorry but this is going to be a really simple and obvious statement: before you start any journey you must know where you want to go. When you jump into a taxi, what's the first question the driver asks?

"Where to guv?"

Imagine their reaction if you said "I don't know, just drive around."

What if you jumped in your car now and started to drive? Where to? Nowhere, just drive. How difficult would that be? It would serve no purpose and would be a waste of time and energy.

Here's the thing.

Every day you jump out of bed and you get into your business, do you really know where you want to go? Where do you _really_ want to take your business?

And if you don't know where you're heading, how will you know if you're going in the right direction?

This is one of the fundamental reasons you've fallen out of love with your business:

"You've lost sight of WHY"

When you started your business you had big plans, you had goals and milestones, you wanted to 'smash 'em out of the park'.

In fact, the chances are you've really worked your arse off to achieve what you've already achieved. And now, x number of years later, your business and your life have changed. As your business has grown its needs and goals have changed, its industry has changed, and customer requirements have changed.

"Death, Taxes and Change (and a sale at DFS)...the only things guaranteed in life".

When you first started the business you had a clear vision, destination and journey mapped out. You may have even had it all written down and occasionally you went back to it. Now, there's a very high chance that you haven't looked at it for quite a while.

What's happened now is you've got sucked into the day-to-day running of your business. You've got a To-Do list somewhere with a heap of great things listed. Each weekend you decide,

"Right, next week I'm going to get some of those important items ticked off my list." You get to work on Monday and get sucked into the vacuum, firefighting everyone's problems, because only you know how to, and then it's Saturday. Another week gone by.

Without realising it you and your business have changed a lot. You've lost sight of why you started this business and what you want out of it… and if you don't know, how do you expect your team to know?

Something has got to change.

> *"If you always do what you've always done, you'll always get what you've always got."*

> Henry Ford (one of my favourite sayings as it's so true.)

There's another really important consideration you need to know and acknowledge before moving on.

In life, the journey is more important than the destination.

Like you I'm really driven, I thought it was all about achieving the goal or getting to the destination. You have to suffer the pain to enjoy the fruit. But when you stop and really think about it, that's not the case.

I enjoy pushing myself both mentally and physically. I never stop learning, and I like to stretch my comfort zones. I've run the London Marathon three times, cycled hundreds of miles on my bike and, of course, all of it at times really hurts. It's hard work and you have to stay focused on your goal to remind yourself of why you're doing it. Sometimes it would be quite easy to say "not today."

But I wouldn't do any of it if I didn't enjoy it, at least at some level.

And it's the same with you and your business, you've got to enjoy it. If not, why do it? What's the point of having the stress and risks of running your own business if you don't enjoy it. Why do it?

Our first principle for Falling Back In Love with Your Business is: **The Journey Is More Important Than The Destination.**

You've got to enjoy the journey.

The first chapter of this book is all about Strategy. It's going to lay the foundation of everything we do from here on, and we're going to create three key plans:

1. Personal Ambition Plan – your personal plan which will identify your ambition, aligned to your values, purpose and lifestyle goals.

2. 5 Year Business Plan & Goals – the strategic goals and tactics required to deliver your business success.

3. Your Fun Plan – for you to get back to enjoying your role and having fun.

By creating and implementing these three plans you will enable the change you need to make to get your journey back on track, and to put that smile back on your face.

Personal Ambition Plan

We already agreed above that without knowing your own personal destination, you're on a road to nowhere. Granted, you may have a good grasp of it in your head but without having it written down, it doesn't count. When you get stuff written down and out of your head:

- You'll get a lot more clarity;

- You can share it with others;

- There's a stronger sense of ownership and accountability;

- You can review, reflect and rewrite (Better Never Stops).

We're going to get these out of your head by creating your Personal Ambition Plan in three steps:

Step One: Personal VIP Statements – Values, Income and Purpose

Step Two: Exit Plan

Step Three: Personal Vision Map

Personal VIPs

In order to complete the Personal VIPs (Values, Income and Purpose statements) you'll first need to complete the Personal Ambition Questionnaire. The purpose of the questionnaire is to 'trash' out your thoughts and the Personal VIPs becomes a summary for you to reflect back on in the future. This is the same process and templates I use with my clients. You can download it by going to www.betterneverstops.global/tools

You can jump direct to the Personal VIPs and miss out the questionnaire, but I've found from experience that your statements won't be as powerful or have the same depth of clarity.

To complete this questionnaire properly, I always encourage my clients to do it away from work and in at least a semi-relaxed state. Perhaps with a glass of wine. Some of my clients worked through it like an interview with their spouse or partner playing the role of the Interviewer asking the questions and taking notes. It's important you take the time to invest in this step. There's real power and purpose if you take the time to sit and reflect. But we need to dig deep and the deeper we go inside your mind and soul, the better and more effective the outcome will be. Some of my clients have had real 'light bulb' moments and a clarity of thought and realisation of what they want to achieve.

The questions are quite straightforward but I'll take you through each one.

My Values

What are the most important things in my life? I want you to think about the bigger stuff. There are some really obvious ones but keep digging, there are no wrong answers.

Why are these important to you? Think about each of the above and write a sentence "this is important because… "

We're going to go a bit deeper. When you leave this world, what do you want to be remembered for? Imagine your family, friends, best friend, spouse or partner, children standing up at your funeral and saying a few words. What would you want them to say and why? Sorry, I told you we need to go deep...

Therefore what do you want your legacy to be, what do you want to leave behind? If money wasn't an issue, what would it be? Think big. What's stopping you?

How does this fit into your business? If it doesn't how could it? Or how could you channel some of your energy in making this happen?

My Income

What is your current income level? Are you happy with this level?

What do you want it to be in 3/5/10 years' time?

How do you believe you can achieve this?

What's stopping you from doing it now?

What would you use this income to do? What's it going to fund? Think big. How does it relate to your values above?

My Purpose

On a day-to-day basis, what is it you love doing the most?

What did you love to do that you don't do any more or don't do enough of?

I want you to imagine looking in your work diary and seeing a week laid out before you that would make you think "Wow, I can't wait to get into work, next week is my perfect week." What would be booked in? What would make you go 'wow'?

What's stopping you having your perfect work week?

What really frustrates you about your business? What really frustrates you about your normal week?

What do you hate doing and why?

If money wasn't an option, what would you spend a blank business cheque on?

I want you to now think about your personal life. After your perfect work week, you look in your diary to find you're taking a week off, away from the business… your time. It's all been booked for you by your 'inner good self'. Again you go "Wow, what a week that will be." What would that week be filled with? What's stopping you doing it?

If you were given a blank personal cheque, so you were now financially free, what would you do now? Think big. Would you carry on with your business or go and do something completely different? Why would you do this or these things?

Ideally, what is your long-term goal?

When do you want to do these things?

How much income or financial fund would you need to do it?

How would/could you fund it?

What other personal goals do you have? What else is on your bucket list?

Now you've written all of these down, I suggest you wait at least a day before completing the next step, which is to fill out the Personal VIPs. Again you can download this template from our website, www.betterneverstops.global/tools.

Personal VIPs (Values, Income and Purpose Statements)

Using your completed questionnaire, you can complete the Personal VIPs. These statements in most cases are summaries of the questions in the questionnaire. Again I'll take you through each statement.

My Values

What are the most important things in my life?

On my passing, what do I want to be remembered for?

And my legacy will be…?

This is because my core values are…?

My core values are reflected in my business by…?

My Purpose

What I love doing most is…?

What stops me doing it is…?

What really frustrates me is…?

What I hate doing most is…?

If money wasn't an issue I would…?

My long-term goal is to…?

I want to do this (when)…?

I would need this much income/financial pot to allow me to do it…?

I'm going to fund this by…?

My other key personal goals are…?

I'm going to achieve these when…?

But for me to achieve them I need to…?

My Income

My income now

What I want it to be within 3/5/10 years

I'm going to achieve this by…?

Exit Plan

"Begin with the end in mind"

7 Habits of Effective People by Dale Carnegie

Would it surprise you to find out that 80% of businesses put up for sale do not sell? (Clinton Lee, UKBusinessBrokers.com)

Why do you think this is?

According to EvolutionCBS the top four reasons are:

1. Lack of preparation

2. Poor financial reports

3. Over-reliance on the owner

4. Unrealistic price aspirations

I don't want you making the same mistakes. The overriding issue above comes down to a lack of strategy and preparation by the business owners.

And of course your biggest fear will be that you don't get the right value for your business on exit. Imagine selling your house or car and only getting half of the expected value.

Your exit may be years ahead and not even remotely on your radar, but it's like all the things you've been told about pension planning. Don't leave it to the year before you retire to decide to put a plan together. There are some actions that, without knowing it, can have a fundamental impact on the value of your company and how you exit it.

I'll take you through what your possible exit options are and the pros and cons of each option. I'll also share with you what the key drivers are that will enhance the value of your business.

Exit Options

On our website www.betterneverstops.global/tools you can download the full table to explore your options. I'll take you through a summary here:

Liquidation/Winding Up Immediate or Over Time: Close and sell the business assets. You can take money out over a period of time, not invest in the business, cash in the assets and close. If you are the sole owner/fee earner this might be only option. Can be fast but with little financial gain.

Keep the Business in the Family: Pass ownership onto family, keep your legacy alive and provides income/job for heirs.

Sell the Business to Managers/Employees: Current employees and/or managers may be interested in buying your business.

Sell the Business in the Open Market: Straight sale to open market. To maximise business value it must be in the best position to sell.

Sell to a Competitor: Position your business to sell to a competitor. Normally themost valuable option, they have the most to gain if done right. If their only motivation is remove some competition, they may close after purchase, thus employees may lose jobs.

Managed Business – Retain Ownership: Option to put daily control to manager/management team and owner continues to have controlling share and continuation of income. This can be within a full sale plan, i.e. put management team in place whilst full potential/buy found

Which of these options most appeals to you?

Personal Vision Map

The last step of your Personal Ambition Plan is creating your Personal Vision Map. This will be the most powerful step in the process and is going to be something you're going to use every day.

As a young manager I read a good many books as I tried to understand my new world of managing people and wanting to keep learning.

I think I first came across the concept after reading 'Think & Grow Rich' by Napoleon Hill some years ago. His teachings are about visualising outcomes in the same way a golfer, footballer or rugby player would think, leading up to the moment they are about to strike that important shot.

When working with clients, I needed something to help them visualise their goals, values and purpose. Just writing them down alone wasn't enough and wasn't powerful enough. They weren't ever going to read or reflect on them every day. Therefore I had a bit of a 'eureka' moment one day. I remembered seeing my close friends Andy & Alison's big world map they had in Andy's home office. They love to travel and on this map had started to plot all the places they had been and, more importantly, the places they wanted to visit. Andy used it as a motivation tool to work hard so that he and Alison could tick the places off they had visited as they travel the world together.

And that was it...How about a motivation wall, your very own Personal Vision Map (PVM)?

I've used this for myself and just about every client I work with, and I can tell you it's tremendously powerful. If you use it well, by keeping it in your mind's eye, its subliminal message will keep you on track and motivated. I encourage my clients to use it as their 'sounding boards', the place they can go to, to quietly reflect and refocus on what's important, why they are doing it and what needs to get done.

Here's how to create yours. You will again need step away from your business, set yourself an evening or time over the weekend to create your Personal Vision Map (PVM). You'll find the answers in the work you've done above (Personal VIP & Exit Plan).

You're going to create an 'as big as possible' mural or picture wall. There are two important rules for your PVM:

1. It needs to be big.

2. It needs to be somewhere you'll see it most days. It can't be hidden away otherwise you won't see it. It's going to be quite personal, that's why it's best to have it somewhere at home. One of my clients has it inside a dart board type cabinet on his office wall and on occasion he will open the doors to sit and reflect on his PVM.

Using all of the things you've thought about in your VIP & Exit above, I want you to think about how you have or can visualise these things:

Adrian Peck

- Your personal goals

- Your values

- What's important to you

- Your core values

- Your exit

- Your big purpose

- Your legacy

How would you visualise each of these? What images come to your head when you read these out to yourself?

Now go on Google (other search engines are available) and find images that best represent your thoughts and print them off to create your PVM. Get really powerful images that strike you. When you stand back to look at the whole I want it to have an emotional effect on you. Stir you deep inside. The more emotive the images, the more powerful this is going to be. Trust me, this is going to be such a powerful tool that it will lift you to places you didn't think were possible. It will help you achieve your goals. It will keep you motivated. It will give you more reason when you've had a dark day. This is going to be your "go to place".

Nothing motivates us more than images.

I've run three London Marathons. The hardest thing about running them isn't the day itself, that's the best bit. The hardest by far is all the hours you spend putting in the miles during the winter, running 40 to 60 miles a week in the freezing wind and rain. Whenever I needed motivation, either to go out or when I was running, in my mind I would picture running towards Buckingham Palace and the Mall. Seeing the Palace, the fountain, the flags, the noise of the crowd, the famous finish line and the medal. It kept me focused on my WHY, the BIG goal.

What is your Buckingham Palace?

What keeps you motivated? Make it personal.

Go to www.betterneverstops.global/tools to see an old example of mine.

I did this exercise with one of my clients, Steve. Steve has a passion for light aircraft, flying models etc. During this exercise, he said, "I'd really like to learn how to fly a plane." So I asked, "what's stopping you?"

"Time, I just don't have the spare time to put into it." Steve runs a £3m turnover packing company, has a family, a dog and a large garden, and so on. Weekend time is very limited and it's difficult to find four hours plus for a flying lesson.

When I first started to work with Steve he had all the classic symptoms of a burnt out entrepreneur. He was working silly hours and had lost focus on why and what this was all about, but we put it on his Personal Vision Map and talked about freeing up every Friday afternoon to devote to learning to fly. We discussed why currently he couldn't free up that time and set about tackling those blockers.

Through the process we worked through Vision and Values and strengthened the team around him, empowering them to be responsible for their roles.

A couple of months went by and Steve started taking every Friday afternoon off to pursue his passion for flying. A couple of months later we were having a catch-up meeting. "So how's the flying going?" I asked.

Steve beamed. "Last Friday I safely completed my first unaided landing."

With a bit of focus, what can you put on your PVM to make it all worthwhile? What's your flying lesson?

5-Year Business Plan & Goals

The final part of this section is your five-year business plan and goals.

The very thought of writing a five-year business plan is probably bringing you out in a cold sweat. You have visions of a huge 100-page document you have to wade through, with graphs and pie charts and deep research.

"It's going to take me weeks to write and will never be read or looked at again!" I hear you scream.

I've got some really good news. How would you feel if I gave you a format and process that could enable you to write a 5-Year Business Plan in just 4 hours and it fitted on one sheet of paper? Granted, it's a big piece of paper.

This one-page plan is put up in your office and like your PVM, will keep your plan always in mind and in sight.

If you go to www.betterneverstops.global you can download the template, the My Business SECCESS® Map, and for small post and packing fee, we'll even send you a free large format A0 copy we use with our clients.

In all my years in management and helping businesses, this is probably the single most effective and powerful management tool I've ever seen and used. I'd love to say I invented it, but no I can't claim that. I actually don't know who invented it (and I'm sorry if you're reading this book and it was you. Please get in touch so I can give you the recognition you deserve).

I came across it when delivering the UK Governments Growth Accelerator programme for small businesses. I was given it as an Obit Diagram, a tool to be used within the programme, along with a single page plan which I had seen and used before.

I've made a couple of tweaks to it and expended it out from three to five years and now call it 'My Business SECCESS® Plan'. I use it now with all my clients and I promise you that, with a small amount of pre-work, you can create a quite detailed 5-year plan within four hours. When it's complete it should be put on a wall so it's in your view every day. Most of my clients have positioned it in their office opposite their desk. Each year we review it; strip it down and rebuild it based on what we know now and the targets required to keep on track to the strategic goal.

How do you use it?

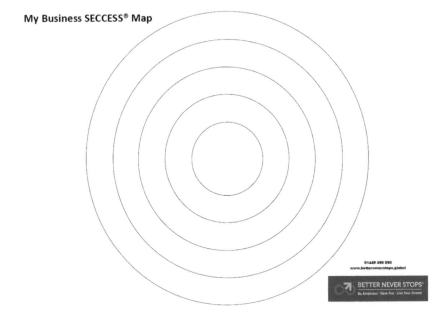

My Business SECCESS® Map

Ideally, you need the large format plan and a number of post-it notes (or similar). You can use different colour sticky squares to represent the different axes if you want. The plan starts from the inside out, with each one representing one year and each line representing the end of the year. The centre circle is this financial year now.

The outermost ring is four years in the future, therefore, including this year, it covers five financial years.

For ease of clarification I'll explain the process, assuming the plan was a clock face, i.e. twelve being at the top, six at the bottom etc.

Pre-Work

Before you can complete "My Business SECCESS® Map" you need to have a clear idea of your business goals and targets. This is a similar exercise to what we did when we explored your own goals and, in some ways, this work will be relevant here.

Your Business Goals

- What is it you want the business to be known for?

- What are its core values?

- Imagine yourself as a potential purchaser of your company, and in five years' time you walked into your business:

  - What would you want to see?

  - How would it have changed from what it is now?

  - How many people would it have?

  - What products would it be selling?

  - What new products has it developed?

  - Would it be across more locations?

  - You speak to some of the staff and you ask them these questions:

- "What's great about this company?"

- "Why do you like working here?"

- "What's different from how it used to be?"

What would you want them to say?

- You meet the Managing Director and you go through some numbers:

  - "What's your turnover?"

  - "How much profit?"

  - "How much are you earning?"

  - "Did you manage to sort out XXX?"

Get a really clear picture in your head and write down your vision of what your company will be like in five years' time. And think BIG, don't be afraid to push yourself and your imagination. What is it you've always wanted to achieve with your business? What's stopping you? If you had the right help and investment in time and/or money where could you take your company and your team? It could be new products, new markets, an acquisition, a partnership etc. DON'T HOLD BACK. This whole process is about getting you working on your business and on what you could achieve if your soul purpose was just to develop the business. If that was all you had to get done every day, week, and month, where could you take it? What could you finally focus your efforts on?

Bear in mind that even if you want to keep it the same size in terms of revenue and team, you'll need at least five to ten percent growth per year to keep up with inflation and rising costs.

You've now got all this written down, a clear idea of what your company is going to be in five years' time.

Let's get started on the My Business SECCESS® Map.

Turnover and Profit

I always start with getting the numbers on the board, by this I mean your turnover and profit aspirations.

On a sticky note, write the turnover figure you want to achieve at the end of your financial year, five years from now and stick it at 'twelve' on the line of the outer ring. Next to it at '1 o'clock' write your desired net profit figure, either as a percentage or as a value.

Within this figure is what you want to earn, as well as what will be retained in the business. This is normally overlooked by many business owners. In order to keep growing (and to stand still you need to grow), the company needs to invest in itself each year to fund the growth, unless you're already sitting on a healthy cash reserve.

If each year you take all the money out of the company, in essence you're likely to starve it of cash, and cash to a company is like oxygen to a human – you will soon notice when it's not there.

Now go to the centre of your Map and on the innermost ring at '12' on a sticky note write your turn-over and profit for this current financial year. If you're less than two months from your year-end use your projected financials for the next year. If you don't know, use what you're likely to achieve this year.

On the rings in between now and the top, write the figure for each year as they step up. For now I would just spread the increase evenly across the years, as we will come back to these as we build the Map. The Map is always a work in progress and that's why we use sticky notes to change or move things about with ease.

If you know your gross profit numbers add these in beside your net profits, along the '2 o'clock' spoke. You may know these aren't great at the moment and that a significant change would increase your overall net profit. Put it in but be aware, as you move around your Map, how you are going to achieve the change in profit; it's not going to happen on its own. Remember Golden Rule #1, only shit happens, everything else you have to make happen.

Okay, that should be all the financial numbers covered for the moment.

This is where the plan starts to come alive. As we stress test the Map, it should ask you lots of questions. Clearly, if growing the company from here to five years' time was easy you would have done it by now. There's a high probability your company, as it stands now, is under-resourced, lacks investment of time and energy and is in a challenging environment – because most are, and if yours wasn't you probably wouldn't be reading this book.

Just stand back for a moment and look at these figures for now and five years' time.

- Is the increase in financials realistic?

- How are you going to achieve it?

- What's got to change?

- What's got to get done?

We're now going to continue this thinking and create a number of spokes to our Map. Each spoke is going to cover a particular aspect of your business and these will be different for each sector or types of businesses. Broadly we'll look at all of these and I'll explain what you need to consider in each. You can decide which are appropriate for your company and include them on your Map. We'll look at:

- Customers

- Marketing & Sales

- Geography or Markets

- Products

- People

- Operations

- Acquisitions

- Investment and Funding

- Partnership or Alliances

- Quality, Regulation or Legal

Of course, most of these aspects are interrelated with one affecting the other. Hence we use sticky notes to change, move or tear up as we continually stress test our Map. Stretching, pulling, testing, thinking...

As you add each spoke carefully consider the knock-on effect to the other spokes. For example, if you launch a new product in year three and therefore you increase sales in year three by £250k, what are the pre- and post-knock-on effects to other spokes?

- Marketing and sales – how and when are you going to generate the new enquiries and sell this new product?

- People – what training or additional resources might be necessary to produce or service this product?

- Finance – is additional funding required to purchase equipment or stock to launch?

- Operations – will this new product have an impact on space or layout to a building?

You don't want your Map to be an 'airy-fairy dreamland wish-list plan'. If it's not realistic you'll never fully buy in to it and soon lose interest in it, with it dying before your eyes and therefore being a complete waste of time. Do it well and it will have a dramatic effect on your life and business, just as your own Personal Vision Map will.

Use the sticky notes on rings to present facts (i.e. numbers) and use the space between each year to describe actions (i.e. gain investors or hire people).

Initially, I would complete the spokes in the order shown above and below as it will make more sense.

Customers

To grow your company from here to five years something has to change with your customers, it has to be either the number of customers, their average revenue, or a combination of these two.

How many customers do you currently serve? Put this number on the innermost ring on a new spoke position, i.e. 3 o'clock.

If you divide your current turnover by the number of customers you'll soon work out your average revenue per customer. Divide your 5-year goal by the average customer revenue number and you'll have the new number of customers you will need to be serving in five years' time. Write this number on the outermost ring. Stand back, and ask, how different is the current level of customers versus the new level?

- How are you going to get these additional customers?

- How will this need to change to hit your five-year goal?

- Will the type or size of customer need to change?

- Are there enough potential customers in your marketplace?

- Can you increase the frequency or the average sales value of your existing customers?

- Do you have a new product up your sleeve that you know your customers would buy from you if you got it launched? How and when will you need to make this happen?

Marketing & Sales

Any changes in customers will inevitably lead to marketing and sales activities. How, what and when do these need to happen? If it's a new product do you have the marketing materials to launch it?

Markets & Geography

Part of your growth plan might be to move into different markets or sectors, or location, in line with your revenue and customer numbers above.

- Can you sell your products to different markets? You might be very trade focused but, with a change in marketing and sales, could you sell to retail customers? Let's say you currently sold catering equipment to restaurants and hotels, could you sell the same products to high-net-worth retail customers?

- What about different parts of your country or different countries? What's holding you back from selling in different locations? If it's only logistics holding you back, why can't you go and find a logistic provider in that location to ship your products?

To make it possible, what needs to happen and when? Is there research or development that needs to happen, and if so when?

Products

In order to hit your 5-year goal:

- Do you have enough products to sell to your existing customers?

- Will any of your current products become obsolete or low margin in five years' time? What effect will this have on revenue and profit? When will they need to be replaced?

- Have you seen an emerging opportunity to sell different products?

- Is there a change in your market through regulation that will require a change in product or a new product?

People

Based on your five-year aspiration, how is this going to affect your team? How many do you employ now? Write this on your 'now' ring. Will the team need to grow? Most businesses rely on people to serve their customers and therefore business growth must lead to more people. You might be over-resourced now, or your current or new products can scale without more people.

If you do need to grow the team, predict when you'll need to recruit and write on each ring your employment and employee count across the years. Inside each ring write the number you need to recruit and perhaps their role, i.e. 2 Admin + 3 Warehouse = 5.

Training

What training will your team need? What year, or years, will this need to be delivered? Is there pending legislation, industry regulation or a change in technologies that your team will need to know? Will the company develop this or use external resources to provide this? Write these actions in the years these need to happen. If you're looking at new products, how will this affect your team?

Operations

Here let's focus on the physical operational aspects like premises, equipment and stock. This is a wide area and any changes from the list above will follow through to operations.

- Will you need to invest in new and/or more equipment, technology or premises? If you're looking at different locations or geography this must follow through to Operations.

- What about process improvements, quality and Health and Safety? We covered some of this topic in "people", but this is more about the physical or asset implications, i.e. buying a new x to meet the required legislation.

- If you're going to expand what about stock, how will this requirement change? More stock requires more space and normally more cashflow to purchase it.

- Will any of your current equipment or plant need to be replaced over the next 5 years? Do you have premises with lease renewals due?

Adrian Peck

Acquisitions

Another growth strategy might be through acquisition of competitors or to enter new markets, locations or countries.

- Is your current market at saturation point such that rapid growth would come from acquiring a competitor?

- Would an acquisition enable you to enter a new market or sector more quickly? For example, you don't have to spend time and money trying to work it out, X Company are already there?

Investment and Funding

As I've stated earlier, businesses need cash to grow. If you're looking at any sort of growth it will need investment. Investment here is twofold: time and money. The company will need to invest time to make things happen and money to fuel the growth. Investments you might need to consider:

- Lower profits while the team focuses on market or product development, or extra people and resources while in development

- Replacement of old or new equipment or plant to develop or produce new products

- Replacement or new software or IT infrastructure to achieve changes in technology

- Setting up new locations or premises

- Marketing and sales activities, i.e. new websites, advertising campaigns or overseas trade events

How are you going to fund any investments? If you're going to fund them from company time build this into your profit forecast. If you need to get funding externally how and when will you need to get the process started? From experience, large funding can take months to arrange.

Partnership or Alliances

A softer and less risky option for expansion might be to form partnerships or alliances with others. Partnerships are an area many businesses overlook and can be a very powerful strategy. We'll cover more on partnerships later in this book when we come to Scale. But is there an ideal partner who you could work with to enter a new sector or market or country?

Quality, Regulation or Legal

Are there any changes on the horizon for your industry? Will there be any knock-on effects from the point above to your legal or regulatory requirements? What about accreditations? If you want to serve a particular type or size of customer will you need accreditation or approval to do business with them? This is often the case when dealing with government organisations. For example, you might be looking to sell your software or IT solution into the UK National Health Service but in order to do so you need to meet their very strict IT accreditation process before you can even enter discussions.

This isn't an exhaustive list and you might come up with other key spokes for your map.

The most important thing is to keep challenging yourself. Most things you put onto your map will have a consequential effect; think it through, keep asking yourself, how will this affect other spokes?

The initial process will take about four uninterrupted hours. Once completed, sleep on it and return to it. I suggest you have someone you can trust to talk through your Map with. Explain to them what it is and how each piece fits together. Get them to challenge you. Just by reading it aloud you'll get more clarity and insight to your plan.

Remember, this is a living, breathing plan, the whole idea is to use it live and constantly re-evaluate at regular intervals.

Vital Few – Single Page Plan

Moving on from My Business SECCESS® Map, the final stage is to produce your Vital Few – Single Page Plan (SPP). This is exactly as it says, a single page plan. Its purpose is to drive the actions required to achieve results in your map. Rather than create an enormous list of 'to do's', we just take the 'vital few' actions that will get you to the next stage. What do you need to do to get from the centre circle (this year) to the next ring (next year)? What are the vital actions you must take?

HOWS			
VITAL FEW (WHATS)	Create/Agree a specification for new site	Work with Agents to find potential sites	Visit shortlist & negotiate final choice
	1	2	3
Outgrown current site – need to move into larger premises by March 2021	#	#	#
Measure	Specification Signed-off	Shortlist Properties	Contract Terms Agreed
Target	May 2020	July 2020	Dec 2020

To download a blank copy of the Vital Few Plan – Single Page Plan, go to www.betterneverstops.global/tools.

The main part of the plan is made up of four key rows and across the page a series of columns that intersect the rows. The rows are your 'WHATS', i.e. what you have got to get done. The columns are your 'HOWS', i.e. how you are going to get the 'WHATS' done.

Let me just explain the process with a simple example.

Vital Few = Outgrown current site – Need to move into larger premises by March 2021. You'll notice this is a SMART objective

(Specific, Measurable, Attainable, Relevant and Timely). Please ensure your Vital Fews are SMART, otherwise the process will be weak and meaningless. For more information on SMART Objectives please see my blog, 'So You Think You're SMART' by visiting www.betterneverstops.global/blogs.

To achieve our Vital Few (our WHAT), we need to a complete three HOWS:

1. Create and agree a specification for a new site. The Measure, i.e. how we know when this is complete, is the Specification Signed-off. The Target, i.e. when we are looking to have this done by, is May 2020.

2. The second step is Work with Agents to find potential sites. Measure = Shortlist Properties. Target = July 2020.

3. Our third HOW is Visit shortlist & negotiate final choice. Measure = Contract Terms Agreed. Target = Dec 2020

A simple test to see if your SPP works is to read your HOWS for a single row and ask, "If you completed these HOWS, would you fully achieve the WHAT?"

If you read through the example table above, each one of the HOWS would logically move you towards finding new larger premises. Therefore by doing the HOWS, the WHAT (Vital Few) will look after itself.

Why the Vital Few?

You'll notice we only have space for a maximum of four Vital Fews (WHATs). This is done purposely to make the plan lightweight and achievable within a realistically short timeframe, i.e. less than a year.

I've worked with management teams with very long shopping lists of live projects (one had as many as 50 between six managers.). Not surprisingly nothing gets achieved because you can't focus on 50 projects at once. Everyone becomes overwhelmed, saying "Where do I start?", and project review meetings become long drawn out affairs with loads of excuses for why people haven't made progress. Of course, these projects are normally done alongside people's day jobs. It's no wonder they fail to get completed and implemented.

By focusing on just a few at a time the plan is more achievable and manageable. Ideally, the WHATs should be broken into small one to two month steps. Once you get these done, create the next ones. This way you build momentum and a habit of positive achievement which will keep everyone motivated and engaged.

Completing Your SPP

Your SPP should focus on the important WHATs within the inner ring of your Map (this year). These are the things you need to get done today which will enable the business to progress to the next ring of your Map (next year). What are the most important things you've got to get done to progress to the next year? Build these up using the template I've provided. You'll notice that some WHATs and HOWS are interdependent and you can mark these within the cross sections with:

* Where the HOW is relevant to the WHAT

0 When the HOW contributes to the WHAT

Leave it blank if it doesn't contribute at all.

Once this is finished, and each HOW has been assigned to a relevant person to champion, the SPP now acts as a Vital Few project managing tool. I would encourage that the relevant people meet weekly (it only needs to be for a short time) and give an update on their progress. Each HOW can be updated using the RAG status (Red Amber Green).

Your Fun Plan - Putting The Smile Back In To Your Role

As we've already established, one of the prime reasons you've fallen, or are falling out of love for your business is because you've lost the fun. Your business has turned into a job, and as an entrepreneur, that's not what it should be about.

As we've already agreed in the introduction to this book, you're in the top 3% of businesses and you're there for a reason. You're driven, highly motivated and prepared to take risks. You're also someone who needs goals and a strategy.

You've got to an age and a point in your life when time has a higher value to you. I'm sure, like me, you've realised by now how precious life is, and how quickly it can change. What's the point in spending eight or more hours every day working so hard doing something you're not enjoying, something that really frustrates you?

You're in control. You own and manage your company. When you look back to why you got into this business, one of your key reasons was that you wanted to be in control, to sail your own boat. Without these important foundations you will continue to be in a "boat to nowhere", and every day you will be a further step away from where your heart truly wants to be.

It's why our first principle is so important.

The Journey Is More Important Than The Destination

In the first step of this chapter we looked at your personal goals; we explored your values, purpose and perfect work week. We also identified what's stopping you having your perfect work week.

Using the answers from your Personal Ambition Questionnaire, I want you to create your own 'Fun Plan' by writing a list of all the stuff you find fun to do in your business and all the elements you dislike doing. Ask yourself, how can I do more of what I find fun and less of what I dislike? You'll find a template at www.betterneverstops.global/tools – Your Fun Plan – Putting The Smile Back Into Your Role.

On the first page you'll find two columns, one for Like Doing and another for Dislike Doing. Write down all the things you like doing in your business and underneath, what stops you doing these things. Under Dislike Doing, write the things you dislike doing and then why you do them.

On the second page create your plan. In the first column complete the rows of "These are the things I'm going to STOP doing". Against each row, who's going to do them instead? When are you going to pass them over? In the next block write the list of tasks or things you're going to do more of or start doing. Against them, when are you going to do them?

Within these steps, involve your team, firstly to make it known (kind of announcing it to yourself) and secondly, to ask their help and hold you accountable to make it happen. There's a very high chance the stuff you find fun is also the stuff you're best at doing. Therefore, why wouldn't you want to do more of it? And your team probably want you to do more of it. There's also a high chance the stuff you dislike doing frustrates your team when you do it.

Your Monthly 'Fun' Check

I want you to now go to your diary and put an action for 30 days' time: Fun Check. In 30 days time you WILL go back to your Fun Plan to reflect back to see how much of your plan you actually achieved. What progress have you made? What columns can you tick Complete (✓)?

If you're not pleased with the outcome, make your Fun Check weekly, every Monday.

You owe it to yourself to have fun, so make it happen!

Strategy Summary

The idea of this chapter is to lay the foundation to build upon for the rest of this book. You must have a well-thought-through strategy that's true to your values and goals. Without it, you and your business will be in conflict. And without a destination the journey becomes pointless and a waste of effort.

Hopefully you've found this chapter quite tough and challenging, particularly creating your Personal VIP Statements.

There's a high chance it's been a while since you asked these types of questions of yourself and your business. It's deliberately tough and hopefully they have made you stop and think about what you are all about and what you really want to achieve. You're not alone, my clients find this step hard work but they get great insights and clarity from this process. Don't leave it here. Use your Personal Vision Map as your daily visual reminder of your why, your monthly 'Fun Check' to make sure you're doing the stuff you enjoy, and at least every year review the whole process again.

And it's the same for you 5 Year Business Plan & Goals. My Business SECCESS® Map is your visual reminder of what the business is aiming to achieve and the Single Page Plan will keep you and your team focused on the actions required to achieve the 5 Year Plan. Most of my clients have their SECCESS® Map on a wall in their office for them and everyone else to see. This way, they can continually sense check their actions today and keep them on course and on track.

EMPOWERMENT

"Coming together is a beginning; keeping together is progress; working together is success."

Henry Ford

I've called this chapter Empowerment because it's about empowering your team. I could have very easily called it Teamwork but I felt that wasn't strong enough on its own (and it really wouldn't have worked for my SECCESS® model).

My goal by the end of this chapter is to have taken you through a series of steps that will enable you to empower your team so that they have more freedom, control, responsibility and rewards.

Just the sound of some of these words will have you coming out in a cold sweat, but in order to Fall Back In Love With Your Business, you'll need principle number two:

You'll Only Achieve Exceptional Results Through Effective Teamwork

To achieve this you have to put a successful team around you. Business is a team sport. Every successful business is only successful because of the teamwork that happens. Read any entrepreneur's book and they will tell you about the key people who have enabled their business success. Managing people is hard work. It's the single hardest aspect of growing a business. Get it right and the rewards are off the scale, get it wrong and every day will be a nightmare.

Here are eight of the most frequent 'people' issues I hear from business owners. See if you recognise any of these:

1. X doesn't do their job right, they used to be so much better.

2. I know I need to delegate more, but I tried it a few times and it just took me longer, and it wasn't done as well as I would have done it.

3. My staff don't share the same passion for the business as I do.

4. My staff don't seem to care as much as I do.

5. Why can't they think for themselves? I'm constantly being interrupted with minor questions they could resolve themselves.

6. Sometimes I get really cross with them when they haven't done what I asked them to do.

7. At times it feels like I'm managing a playground full of kids.

8. Why do some people just do the bare minimum? It wouldn't hurt them to just step it up once in a while.

Do any of these sound familiar to you?

There's a couple of unwritten rules you must accept when managing people who work for you:

1. They don't care as much about your business as you do and they never will. Get over it. Sorry to be so harsh but they won't, it's not their baby. This is their job and you are the boss.

2. You can't manage people through your own eyes, i.e. assuming they have the same work ethic and approach as you. If they did, they would be running their own business.

Once you accept and acknowledge these two unwritten rules, managing people becomes a lot easier. By the way, this doesn't make them bad people, far from it. We are all different and you must manage people through their eyes to get the best from them. We all have a role to play, and when I work with clients, I get them to think about their business as an orchestra.

An orchestra is a collection of many types of instruments and players assembled into four main sections, Strings, Woodwind, Brass, and Percussion. Each plays a key role in performing a music score delivered as close to perfect as possible for their expectant audience.

An orchestra is led by a Conductor, who unifies the players, sets the tempo and listens critically to control the interpretation and pacing of the music so that the score is delivered how they want it interpreted.

Where does a conductor stand and why? Of course at the front so that they can see the whole of their team, they have full visibility of what's going on and they can direct them accordingly.

Have you ever seen a conductor get down from their stand to take over an instrument? What would happen if they did?

Let's look at a business. It has a collection of people divided into sections, according to their job task. Each plays a key role in getting an order delivered as close to perfect to delight their expectant customer.

So who's their conductor?

Yes it's an analogy but hopefully you can see how this is your role in your business, you are the conductor. Like you, a conductor knows how to play an instrument to a high level, they have a working knowledge of the technical aspects and know what it's like to play. But they trust their team to deliver what's asked of them. When you see an orchestra play it's very easy to forget the hours of practice that have gone into performing that piece. The Conductor would have spent time with each section and with an individual player getting them to understand what they need to achieve and their role in helping the orchestra achieve it.

In the same way your team needs to understand what the vision of the business is, their role and responsibilities to get it delivered and what success looks like so they know when they have achieved it.

By stepping out of the day-to-day and empowering your team you'll see improvements and opportunities so much clearer.

Adrian Peck

But 'hang on to your hats, it's going to be a bumpy ride'. After all, you're an entrepreneur who likes to be in control, you're a perfectionist and don't like delegating. Before going forward we have to agree on one really important thing.

These are the great qualities that got you where you are today. They are also the qualities that are now holding you back. In order to fall back in love with your business and live your dream, you've got to get past these and empower your team.

Yes it's scary, I know I might as well have asked you to cut off a toe. The good news is that I have some proven steps I'm going to take you through which, if implemented, will enable you to empower your staff.

Throughout this chapter, I'm going to refer back to the orchestra and conductor model. It's a great example of a leader working in harmony with their team to achieve a common goal. I believe it represents something we can all relate to and visualise easily.

We're going to cover four main steps.

Step One: Team vision and values. I'm going to help you see the importance and need for a team to share a collective vision and set of values. Like an orchestra, your team needs to know why they're doing it and to realise they want the same thing. I'll also take you through the techniques I use with my clients to create a vision and agree the values.

Step Two: Team Roles and structures. Your company needs a clear structure which defines the key tasks and lines of communication. This is the equivalent of the Strings, Woodwind, Brass, and Percussion sections.

Step Three: Individual responsibilities and objectives. It's easy to see how each player in the orchestra knows exactly what's expected of them and what they need to achieve. It's a simple concept and one you can use in your business to ensure the same happens within your teams.

Y Step Four: Rewards & communication. When an orchestra completes their piece they get their reward; a round of applause, perhaps a review written about them and perhaps a drink backstage or in the local pub together where they can collectively acknowledge a job well done. I'm going to share some simple ways you can ensure that your teams know they've done a good job and how you can reward them.

Team Vision and Values

"Teamwork is the ability to work together toward a common vision."

Andrew Carnegie

One of the most common complaints I have from business owners is of the workforce not caring about the company in the same way they do. Or that the staff don't share the same goals they do.

And I ask them, "When was the last time you sat down with everyone and shared your vision and values with them?"

"Ah, not for a while, mmmm probably never. Oh probably when I interviewed them," comes the reply.

Nothing unifies a team like a common goal. Deeply rooted inside us humans is a sense of belonging, wanting to fit in and having rapport with our fellow human beings. Take this example: You walk down your local high street and you pass a stranger, you might gesture a hello or good morning and carry on your walking. You think nothing of it, there's no common connection or rapport.

Place the two of you on a bus in a far-flung country whilst on holiday and you hear a local accent. You turn and strike up a conversation to find out that you come from the same town and you live a few streets away. You instantly build rapport and now have a common connection.

Look at any successful sports team: the bit that brings them together is their shared vision, values and goals. It's the difference between the good and the great achieving team. Football has a way of proving that a group of talented players doesn't guarantee success on the pitch. In 2016 we witnessed Leicester City Football team win the English Premier League. Arguably there were many teams that season with players more talented than them, but they shared a belief, a common set of values, and a very clear goal. They will be forever immortalised in football folklore as the team that won the Premier League at 5000-1 odds.

Let's go back to our Conductor and Orchestra model. Before they even start to rehearse the Conductor will meet with them to discuss the 'why'. Without the why, what's the point? As in your business, if you think they do it for the money you're miles off. Many orchestras are unpaid groups of musicians sharing a passion and pastime. In your business, pay is important for your team (stop paying them and you'll soon find out), but it's only actually a small factor as to why they work and work for you. So there has to be a collective understanding of why they do what they do and what they want out of it. The challenge for you is how to open up this dialogue with your staff. How do you go from a collection of individuals to a cohesive team?

Vision & Values Workshop

For the businesses I work with I run Vision and Values Workshops, and I'll take you through how I run them and what we look to get out of them.

Having worked for corporate 'blue-chip' companies I've seen my fair share of mission, vision and values statements. Mostly these have been written by 'the board', often using a language only they really understand and always with far too many words, especially for someone dyslexic like me... There was never a connection with the real people, the employees who faced the customers every day. I've seen lists of values sometimes ten or more deep. The point of having values is that everyone agrees with them and strives daily to live and breathe them.

To me, I believe they should be natural and define the personality of the business. Going back to our orchestra, it's the style and interpretation of the music.

I've seen small businesses trying to adopt the same corporate style as large companies with little success. I found so much confusion between a mission and vision statement. What's the difference or the point of both? The values were a string of words the business owner wanted them to be but were far from what the real personality was.

I realised the bit that was missing was that the process had been done by management and not the workers, and therefore the workers didn't buy in to them. They had no ownership, and without ownership, there's no possession. Without getting buy-in from the team things will go horribly wrong. I personally found this out the hard way, and I'll come to that later when I explain how I learnt the importance of teamwork when I created the Mercedes Benz Accident Repair Licenced Technician Scheme.

I had also remembered back to when I was 22-year-old working as an Automobile Association (AA) Patrol. As part of my training, I visited one of the call centres and on entering the building I saw a sign above the door which read:

"You are part of a proud tradition, ensure you do your best to uphold it"

The AA was formed in 1905, so it had a deep history and I certainly felt part of it. Seeing this had a profound effect on me, given that I can still recall it a good few years later.

I knew there had to be a better way for my clients to take that first step in building their cohesive team, so I created the Vision and Values Workshop, an interactive workshop designed to bring everyone from a company together, to create a vision and a set of values they believe in. In the workshop they are going to do three things:

1. Get some frustrations off their chest and realise some of the good reasons they come to work;

2. Create a vision of what they want the business to be achieved or recognised for;

3. Write the values which they believe the company stands for.

Ideally, the workshops need to be run by a facilitator, an independent person who has little connection with the company. This will ensure feedback is given openly, the workshop is not steered in a certain direction and conversations don't run too deep.

Here's the process for the Vision & Values workshops (examples can be found on our website: www.betterneverstops.global/tools):

1. Invite small groups to a workshop. The groups need to be four to eight people and mixed departments. The workshops run for an hour and you'll need a large table for everyone to sit around, a flip chart, normal pens and coloured marker pens, sticky notes (post-it) and a good few sheets of flip chart paper. It should be the whole company, except the owners. Any managers should be divided amongst the groups.

2. The first task is what I call Good Bad & Change. Using the flip chart write the words Good Bad & Change, underneath each other but spaced out down the left hand side.

3. Give each participant three sticky notes and a pen. On the sticky notes they will write:

    a. Good – one thing they really like about working at the company.

    b. Bad –one thing that is bad, a frustration to them that stops them doing their job well.

    c. Change – one thing they'd like to change. If they were given a magic wand, on a Friday they waved it and on

Monday when they returned to work one thing had changed, what would that one thing be?

4. When they have written their three sticky notes, place each on the flip chart under Good, Bad & Change.

5. When everyone has finished, discuss with the group what and why people have written, and any key issues that need further investigation and follow-up post-workshop. Summarise the points raised and move onto the next task.

6. They are now going to create a shield or a coat of arms that represents and visualises what they want the company to be in the future. They're only allowed to put a maximum of four words on it (plus the company name). These words should be the values they feel are important to them and are what they want the company to be recognised for. To create it they need a sheet of flip chart paper and the coloured marker pens. They have 30 minutes to complete the task. They'll need to take a few minutes to plan out what they might want to create. I would encourage them to come up with their values first.

7. We normally add an element of competition to the shield creation by awarding the team who creates the best shield a fish & chip or pizza lunch. This just gives it extra spice and encourages more participation by adding the common goal.

8. Post-event I would meet with owners and managers to:

    a. Summarise and discuss the feedback from Good Bad Change and agree on the follow-up actions. These follow-up actions are important as an opportunity to show you care and build trust with the team. Use this opportunity wisely.

b. Hang the shields up around the meeting room and discuss the values that have been shared. Agree what the three or four key company values will be.

c. Discuss the visual representation of what's been created and the meaning of them and use it to create a vision statement.

d. Agree on the winning shield and discuss the overall elements in creating a professionally designed shield to become the company's internal coat of arms

e. Fix a launch date to present the winning shield and the new company vision, values and coat of arms. We normally do this over lunch-time and provide everyone with fish & chips or pizza as a celebration.

9. The professionally designed shield with the vision and values gets printed onto foam boards and, after the launch, they are displayed on as many walls as possible around the company. In one of my client's premises, a large logistics company in Suffolk, they have three values: Integrity, Commitment & Excellence. We had each word printed in a different colour and the text transposed vertically and put onto large boards. At the end of each racking aisle a word was hung so that when you walked into a building you really couldn't fail to see them.

In reality, this is just the start of the vision and values process. Your responsibility is to embed these into your culture so that they live and breathe in your business every day.

My job in this book is to enable you to **fall back in love with your business**. Managing people is hard work but the first step is to get them all pulling in the same direction. If we think back to our Conductor and Orchestra analogy, Vision & Values is just agreeing what music we're going to play and the style in which we're going to do it.

The purpose of having the Vision & Value boards around the business is to daily keep them in everyone's peripheral vision to remind them about what you're trying to achieve and how they are expected to behave. Remember these were chosen by them, they are their values. Your job is to now ensure they work to these values and the easiest way to achieve this is by working them into your company culture and habits. Here are a few ways you can do it:

- Employee incentive scheme (we'll come back to this under rewards and communication).

- Include them in your recruitment process so that new employees are aligned to your values from day one. Assess candidates against your values and, at interviews, ask them for examples of how they have displayed the values in previous roles.

- Use them in your appraisal process, we call them LOVED: Living Our Values Every day. Go to www.betterneverstops.global/Tools and you'll find a template for conducting LOVE reviews.

- Get them on the agenda of team and individual meetings. "One of our values is quality, last week we achieved…" or "John, can you explain how your behaviour is in line with our values?"

- Include them in all written employee communications; staff notices, emails, training etc. Use different letter header and email footers for internal communication with the vision and values.

The intention of the workshops was to break the ice and give you an opportunity to start something new and fresh, 'shake it up a bit'. You and your team's responsibility now is to make it happen.

Team Roles and Structures

If we go back to our Conductor and Orchestra analogy, the orchestra has a clear structure. Players and their instruments are put into sections and each section plays together to give the sound volume and depth.

In your company you need people organised into sections so that it can efficiently and effectively deliver your customers' needs. You may think, "we already do this, Tom and Sally look after customer orders, John does the invoicing etc etc…"

From my experience what easily happens in growing companies is that they lose their structure. Over a period of time they become responsive to what needs to get done today and trapped in the habit of 'fire fighting'. This is your opportunity to take a step back to ensure your company hasn't been sucked into that trap.

I also want to introduce the concept of building your structure for the company you want tomorrow and not just to serve its needs today.

If you want to really develop and grow your business, get your structure built for tomorrow so it will lift it up and not hold it back.

Key Structure

This may feel rather obvious or basic but I don't want to just assume you've got this covered. For most businesses this is the simplest form a successful company should have:

- A Leader, most often the business owner

- Sales Manager, responsible for generating the sales orders

- Operations/Customer Service Manager, responsible for getting your sales orders turned into happy customers

- Finance Manager, responsible for money in, money out and reporting the financial results

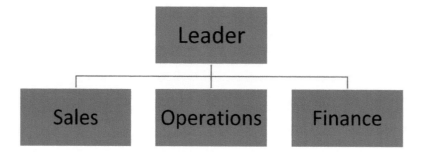

For some types of 'sales organisations' like Estate Agents and Recruitment Agents, this structure gets a little fuzzy because the sales and operations happen within the same role. For example an estate agent, normally the salesperson, engages with the seller and sells their house. In these instances I would replace sales with 'New Business', which is someone solely responsible for generating new sales, and operations in the combined sales/customer service role.

The importance of this structure is that you have a single person at the top and three people responsible for achieving Sales, Operations & Finance. I have worked with clients who have been a partnership or a group of three or four directors/equal shareholders, and they have all tried to be the Leader. Seldom have I seen this work successfully.

You need to have a leader. The leader doesn't get sucked into all the details of the day-to-day. They need to be the conductor and they make decisions from standing out in front. How could a conductor playing in the brass section be able to hear the tempo and lead the orchestra?

As a £1-million-plus turnover company this should be your structure now. If it isn't, you need to look at putting this in place. You need to make three different people responsible and accountable for delivering these roles. Don't confuse this with merely reporting as they must have the skills and attributes to be able to manage and achieve the desired output of the roles on a monthly basis. If for now the finance manager is not a full-time role, who could fulfil this on a part-time basis? With online banking & accounting software, this person doesn't even have to work in your building.

The next step for the business is to put a structure in place which is going to lift it to the next level. I want you to imagine you and your team of three standing at the bottom of a large rock face. The rock face represents your business and the four of you need to climb to the top. The four of you begin to climb by hammering in the next peg and pulling yourselves up one level at a time. All of a sudden four ropes are dropped down and each of you gets assistance to reach the top with less than half the amount of effort. The assistance came from having a bigger structure than you needed at the bottom.

What structure would lift you up to the next level?

If you want to really develop and grow your business, get your structure built for tomorrow and so it will lift it up and not hold it back.

Your Next Level Structure

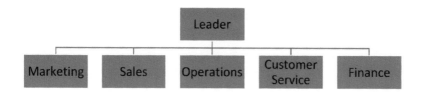

In the example structure above we've added two new sections:

Customer Service – responsible for customer satisfaction within the service/product process stage.

Marketing – responsible for lead generation and assisting with customer maximisation.

The Customer Service role depends on the type of organisation and how you deliver your product/service. It works well if your company makes its products and has a team to install or service the products. It doesn't work so well if your company merely buys in and installs, or manufactures and dispatches a product, because the operational and customer service elements are within the same process. The Customer Service role takes the customer from sales and through the process.

The Marketing or Lead generation is a very important step up role. I've seen many companies who try to combine this into a sales and marketing function, and this never works well unless there is a sales and marketing director with two managers below with separate responsibility.

When marketing and sales are combined into one role, that person inevitably has a strength in only one of those disciplines and the stronger one just becomes a distraction (and often an excuse) from the other.

The Marketing section has two key roles:

1. Responsibility for generating good quality sales leads ready for the sales section to turn into orders.

2. Ensuring the maximisation of every customer through the process and long after the order has been delivered.

It might seem very obvious, but each section should have its role defined, i.e. what they are responsible for day-to-day, weekly, monthly and annually. Working with your team I would suggest creating a simple table like below:

Section	What We Are Responsible For?			
	Day-To-Day	Weekly	Monthly	Yearly
Marketing				
Sales				
Customer Service				
Operations				
Finance				

For the moment just focus on the high-level roles. We'll drill into the task-oriented roles when we look at each section below.

You need to think about who is going to manage some of the compliance-type roles such as Health & Safety, HR etc. For most businesses up to a £5m turnover, I would always recommend outsourcing these to expert consultants with someone from the management team overseeing their implementation. In my experience, these experts live and breathe their specialism every day and they will always be far more efficient and effective than someone trying to learn and keep up to date part-time.

Individual Roles And Responsibilities

The next step is to break your table down into single sections. Working with the section manager and their team (if applicable), identify the individual roles and responsibilities.

Here's how the table might look:

Section Name	Sales	Manager Name	Julie Collins
Task Description	**Measure**	**Target**	**Who Responsible**
Creating sales quotes	*Sent to customer*	*Within 4 hrs*	*John, Katy, Steve*
Quote follow-ups within 1 working day	*Sales conversion*	*57%*	*John, Katy, Steve*
Sales order hand-over to customer service team	*Order received by CST*	*Within 1 hr*	*John, Katy, Steve*

Task Description - You're now going to drill into the detail and, in effect, build a list of key tasks for each section.

Measure – What is the measure for knowing that this task has been completed?

Adrian Peck

Target – What should be the target?

Who's Responsible – put names against the task for who is responsible for getting it done. This should be the person or people who are the most able to complete that task. You need to ignore what's happened previously. "John has always done that task" doesn't mean John is the right person to get the task done for two reasons:

1. Bad habits form over a period of time, and it's easy for people to slip into a comfortable zone of what they like to do versus what needs to get done. I've seen this many times when people are doing a task which has little relevance to what the business needs to achieve.

2. There's a difference between 'getting a task done' and 'doing a task'. One is taking responsibility for ensuring a task has been completed and the other is actually doing the task. This often gets confused by people believing "I've got to get all these tasks done" rather than ensuring the tasks are completed by using a team of people. It's why this chapter is called Empowerment because it is the essence of teamwork. All the way through the company people should be empowered to do a great job.

This is where you start to find out that the roles people do now are quite different from what they were originally employed to do. But it's a chance for the team to refresh. We'll cover this a lot more in the Efficiency chapter where we'll cover the end to end business processes.

In our Conductor and Orchestra analogy, how does each player know what to do?

1. They have a printed sheet in front of them telling them what to play

2. During rehearsals, the conductor has given them feedback and guidance on how they want it played

In your business, give each member of the team a sheet explaining what is expected of them and give them feedback on how they're doing.

Communication And Rewards & Recognition

Communication

Remember, in the Vision & Values workshop the first exercise was to ask all staff to write three things: one really good thing they like about working for you, one really bad or frustrating thing that prevents them from doing a great job, and one thing that if they waved a magic wand on a Friday would be changed on a Monday morning.

I'll have a little side bet with you here. I'll guarantee when you count all of the Good, Bad and Change feedback, the top Bad & Change will be… poor or bad communication. It's happened on every block of workshops I've run. If I'm wrong we'll share a nice bottle of wine on me.

In our Conductor & Orchestra analogy, imagine if the Conductor stopped communicating with the Orchestra?

Here's the thing. During this process you've asked for feedback, you've got people engaged and potentially a little bit excited about the future. You have a perfect platform to keep that momentum going and show people they have been listened to and things are progressing. And as poor or bad communication was their top concern you and your team need to take action. Here's what I suggest you do:

1. Hold a communication improvement meeting. Within each team get them to hold a 15 to 30-minute meeting with just one topic on the agenda: How can we improve communication? This should just be about asking the question not solving it, so make sure they avoid "OK as from Monday we'll now…." If you try to solve it there and then: 1 The meeting could run for hours, 2 You'll lose sight of getting to the issues, 3 You won't necessarily see the bigger picture, and 4 They might make or get drawn into promises they can't keep.

2. Have the same meeting with your section managers, same rules apply, do not slip into solution mode.

3. Find a way to collate the feedback in the same document and format, and have a separate meeting to analyse and discuss the feedback within the teams.

4. You can get into solution mode and identify the key issues you can address and how you're going to address them. Don't discount anything without giving feedback as to why you can't achieve it. Give time frames for when it will be implemented or investigated. Take the opportunity to give feedback to everyone of the findings and solutions, either via a company meeting or smaller team meetings. Also, provide a printed copy for them to digest afterwards.

5. Implement the solutions.

6. Keep the momentum running. Within the teams, get the section manager to provide monthly communication meetings, updating them on the team performance, company performance and company developments. More on this in the next chapter, Control.

Rewards & Recognition

Everyone Likes To Feel Important And Appreciated

According to world-renowned expert in people management Frederick Herzberg's two-factor theory of job satisfaction, people are influenced by two sets of factors, so-called hygiene and motivational factors.

Hygiene factors do not motivate and if they are not there will act as de-motivators. These are factors like level of pay, job security, nice working environments. They don't motivate people to work harder but take them away and they'll work less.

Motivational factors could involve job recognition, rewards, the potential for promotion and having enjoyable work. If workers don't benefit from these factors it will not necessarily lower motivation, but the presence of these factors will increase their motivation.

Therefore if you want your team to work hard, be motivated to come to work and do a great job, make sure you get the hygiene factors right and use the motivating factors to lift them. And most of the time it is that simple.

When I talk to clients about creating reward and recognition schemes within their business, I often see their faces glaze over as they imagine a huge financial burden been placed upon them. But when we discuss a few ideas they soon realise that actually these don't need to cost a fortune.

I'll share with you here a few reward & recognition schemes I use with my clients:

- Verbal praise and thanking people;

- Handwritten note to praise and thank someone;

- Praise in front of team;

- Buying a small gift, flowers or a car wash etc, just something personal you know they would appreciate;

- Let them leave off an hour early;

- Gift voucher or offer to pay for a meal out for them and a friend/partner/spouse;

- A birthday surprise;

- Fish & Chip or pizza Friday for all staff or a team.

I'm sure you get the idea. None of these are high cost and the good news is that currently in the UK you can spend £150 per year per employee without any PAYE 'benefit in kind', i.e. not tax and national insurance deductions (just check with your accountant). You also get to reclaim the VAT.

After the launch of Vision & Values, a contract packaging company in Suffolk, rolled out Perkbox to all their staff. It's an online staff reward scheme and, for a small annual subscription, you can provide access to your team. They get to receive a wide choice of benefits: money off vouchers, self-improvement training, medical helpline etc. Via the platform you can also send them rewards and thank you messages and reward icons.

At a logistics company, as part of Vision & Values, we set up a quarterly employee incentive scheme, Vision & Values Star Awards. Managers nominate individuals and teams against the values. Individuals are rewarded with vouchers and teams with a team meal or lunch. At the end of each year, the quarterly individual and team winners are invited to a celebration lunch to announce the individual and team of the year. Each quarter a team 'vision and values themed' newsletter is produced and sent out covering a wide range of news, features and the 'Star Awards' nominations and winners. The entire programme is there to constantly reinforce the company vision and values and is another way of saying thank you and recognising the hard work people put into the team.

Summary

My Mercedes Benz story and why it's so important to get buy-in from your team

To finish off this chapter, I want to share with you the day I found out how important teamwork and getting buy-in from your team is.

Around 2006 I was working for the Carter & Carter Group and at that time they were the largest Automotive Consultancy company in the UK. I was Head of Accident Repair Training and Development Solutions, and most of my role was to work with major vehicle manufacturers to create training programmes for their approved accident repair (or Body Shops) and, through my team, deliver the solutions. Over the course of 18 months to 2 years I had been working with Mercedes Benz (based in Milton Keynes) and their Approved Network (around 200 Body Shops) to provide a training programme to ensure that every Mercedes was repaired to their very high technical standards. Mercedes cars are amongst the most innovative and were often leading the way in terms of advanced safety and construction techniques. Mercedes were very keen to keep the repair of the vehicles within their Network, thus ensuring a brand experience for their customers and protecting parts revenue.

I had worked for months: talking to their Network, the brand, their dealerships, the industry and body shop technicians to put together a training solution. Putting all this hard work together I formulated the Mercedes Benz Accident Repair Licensed Technician Programme, an industry-leading solution taking technicians from 14-years-old into an apprenticeship combined with a structured adult training and competency programme.

Mercedes loved it so much they mandated that every approved body shop had to have at least three Licensed Technicians to meet their Dealer Standards. I presented the whole solution at the Mercedes Benz Accident Repair Conference, and the Network also like my solution. In fact, they quickly signed up and within weeks we had most of the body shops paying £225 per technician per month to join the programme. I was on course to generate over £1.5m per year from this programme. Using the same model, I was talking to other manufacturers about creating a similar programme under their brands. This was developing into a £10m per year opportunity.

It was all going so well until…

I needed the help, support and facilities within Carter & Carter to deliver the programmes. I gathered the key stakeholders together for a meeting to tell this great news and to discuss how we could deliver the programmes. And that's when it hit a brick wall. Basically, they sat and listened attentively and in not so many words said "#### you." They weren't interested in any shape or form. "We haven't got the time or resources" was their excuse. I knew they did, we were having a brand new facility in Derby built and I had been promised by Phil (CEO) we would have dedicated accident repair training centre. But they weren't bothered. I was absolutely wrecked. What made it worse was that we had the new Mercedes S Class launch to the Network within a few months.

Devastated and distraught I met with my boss and explained the situation. He looked and me and said, "But surely they've supported the programme and the concept during this journey?"

And that's when I realised what I'd done. I was so engrossed with MY solution and working with the brand and their network, I had forgotten to involve the team. They didn't buy-in to it, they'd had no involvement, they didn't feel part of it. From here on every day was an internal battle to get the programme delivered.

Hopefully you can see why I wanted to tell you the hard lesson I learnt and you'll see how this relates to you and your business. One of the major reasons you've fallen out of love with your business is due to the hard work of managing people. But business is a team sport.

You'll Only Achieve Exceptional Results Through Effective Teamwork

If you want them to play your tune, you've got to act like a conductor, act like a leader and work in harmony with your team to achieve a common goal.

Use the four steps we covered in this chapter to enable you to engage and implement this philosophy.

1. Team vision and values, the opportunity to create a collective vision and share a set of values so your team knows why they're doing it and to realise the same goal.

2. Team roles and structures giving your company a clear structure to define the key tasks and lines of communication.

3. Individual responsibilities expected of them and what they need to achieve.

4. Rewards and communication so your teams knows they've done a good job and how you can reward them.

You've got to get them to buy in to what you're doing and why you're doing it, make them part of it. Get their hearts and minds connected to you and the business and 80% of the hard work is done. It sounds simplistic but teams working in harmony and with a strong belief are powerful forces. They can defy the odds and even win Premiership Leagues as 5000-1 outsiders. Anything is possible.

CONTROL

"You can't manage what you can't measure. What gets measured gets managed."

Peter Ducker

From the previous chapter we've now built your team up, got them on board with the vision and values and launched a recognition and reward scheme. But there's still one major issue which will hold back your team: they need to know the score.

Everyone in your business should know if they've done a good job. At the end of each working day they should be able to reflect and know if they have achieved what was expected of them. Ideally, because the communication process has been so clear, they know throughout the day how they've performed. At worst, at the end of the day, their line manager or a screen on a wall should be able to tell them if they have achieved the score they were expecting.

If we go back to Herzberg's Two-Factor Theory, one of the key motivation factors is achievement. People are motivated by achievement. I'm sure we can all remember a reward chart at home or school when we were very young and that magical feeling of achievement we got when another sticker or tick went on the chart. It's no different for adults, we're all motivated by achievement and teams are united through a common aim or purpose.

And it's no different for YOU. One of the reasons you've fallen out of love with your business is that you've lost your sense of achievement. You've been dragged into a rut of trying to cope with the day-to-day and lost sight of what you want to achieve and knowing where you are on the journey. That, in turn, makes the journey feel like a constant traffic jam. It goes back to our first core principle, **the journey is more important than the destination.** You've got to enjoy the journey.

Enjoyment comes from having fun doing what you do and the sense of achievement you get from it. To get the sense of achievement you need to know the score. Very few businesses have goals, even less have them written down and track the results.

I don't know if you have ever played a sport, but imagine playing and not knowing the score until the end of the game: until after the final whistle?

Why do this in your business? I've met several businesses that rely on their accountant to tell them their results some six to nine months after the year-end. How can that work well? If you are serious about falling back in love with your business, and driving your business forward, you've got to be good at being results-focused.

I always use the dashboard analogy with my clients. I get them to think of their business as a car with the dashboard giving them constant data, allowing them to make decisions along their journey. How difficult would your car be to drive without a dashboard?

In this chapter I'm going to help you build a dashboard for your business. To be able to do this I'm going to take you through four steps:

Step One: Define the company goals. We're going to identify the key goals that drive your business.

Step Two: Measure the goals. Work out how we can measure these goals, what you're currently achieving and what the future targets should be.

Step Three: Record the score. Create your dashboard to record the goals.

Step Four: Share. Launch and share the goals and dashboard with all the team.

Without a dashboard in your business, you're getting into your car without knowing how fast you're going or how far along the journey you are. And it's the same for your team, they don't know what's expected of them and what the score is.

The next step to fall back in love with your business is based on principle number three: **Know what you want, measure, assess and drive performance**

We're all motivated by achievement and teams are united through a common aim or purpose.

Step One: Define the company goals

In this step it's important we get to the heart of what drives your business success but also to keep it simple.

Simplicity will drive the right performance.

Why? Because if ALL your team know the goals, know the score and know how they can affect the score, you will have a very powerful dashboard.

If you think about a car dashboard, every car has at least three dials: speed, fuel and mileage. Added to this is probably another three: engine temperature, oil pressure and engine revolution counter. In total there's only actually around five to six dials and several warning or indicator lights, i.e. lights on, full beam, handbrake etc.

But you could simply drive a car with three dials. You'd know how fast you're going, how much fuel you've got and how many miles you've covered. And every driver would understand those dials and how they could affect the score and keep legal.

- If I drive faster, I'll cover more miles

- If I drive too fast I might exceed the speed limit

- If I drive faster I'm likely to use more fuel

- If I put more fuel in, I can cover more miles without stopping

I'm sure you get the idea, and hopefully see why it's important to keep it simple. You could very easily add another three dials, and numerous indicator and warning lights, and confuse or complicate the matter for the driver. Or worst still, distract them from what they really need to focus on.

I want you to imagine you're on holiday, lying on a sun lounger on a beach. You're sitting enjoying the sun and the view, with a nice cold drink in your hand. You lay back in with the sun on your face and your mind flicks to think about your business and you suddenly get anxious wondering how their week has gone and if everything is OK. If I allowed you to make a phone call to your company, but you were only allowed to ask three questions to find out how your business was doing, what would those three questions be? What three questions would get you straight to the pulse of your business?

- What would tell you how fast it was travelling?

- What would tell you how much fuel it had used and how much was left?

- What would tell you how far it had travelled?

Let's look at a couple of live examples of businesses I work with, using actual measures but fictional numbers. These would be their live dashboards, looking at a point in time during a month:

Underfloor Heating Design, Supply & Advice – demo live dashboard

- How fast: Enquires 156

- How much fuel: Orders dispatched on-time 100%

- How far: Gross profit £35,000

Windows Doors Conservatories – demo live dashboard

- How fast: Customer leads 56 & Sales orders £165,000

- How much fuel: Installations completed on time 100%

- How far: Sales invoiced = £145,000

Manufacturing company – demo live dashboard

- How fast: Orders dispatched on time 100%

- How much fuel: Units produced 108

- How far: Sales invoiced = £65,000

Your dashboard can be as simple as these. In fact, I urge you to keep it this simple. Try to avoid over-complication otherwise you'll have problems with steps two, three and four below.

What are your three key performance indicators?

- One needs to focus on sales, either sales enquires or sales orders. This depends on your type of business. Do your sales happen straight away (sales orders) or is there a lag of time to convert a customer (sales enquiries)?

- A second needs to focus on order delivery or production or capacity. Again, it depends on your business, but sitting on your beach you need to know if your customers are getting their goods or the factory is making them.

- The last one needs to focus on money, either sales revenue or gross profit.

Simple Dashboard Example

Sales This Month		Operations This Month	
Leads	50	Jobs Completed	50
Orders	£200,000	Invoiced	£190,000

It might be that you've got a very good case of having more than three dials but tread carefully, to keep it simple. Think about your business and which actions drive your goals.

Step Two: Measure the goals

OK, you've got the basis of your main dials in place, you now need to decide three things:

1. How: On a daily basis how are you going to gather the information to put on your dashboard?

2. Current: What results are you currently achieving?

3. Future: What results do you need to achieve your business goals?

These three steps will determine if you've got the dials simple enough, often I find that this is where they fall down.

How

Each day the dials need to be updated. At this point don't get distracted by the technology. I've seen many business owners get all 'techy' trying to find super dashboard tools. Please don't get drawn into this trap. Focus on how someone is going to gather this information daily to update the dials. Don't be embarrassed if you don't currently record this information, I've met many businesses who don't how many sales enquiries they get each day or the value of their sales order book.

Think of this as progress. When you start to record this information, magic starts to happen... read on

Ideally, the gathering of this information shouldn't take more than 5-10 minutes each day. If it's currently not recorded can you instigate a simple recording sheet on someone's desk, i.e write the number of sales leads generated over the phone that day. Keep it simple and people will do it, complicate it and they'll find every reason not to do it. The process and recording of the 'score' is as important as knowing the result.

Creating Targets

Having scores on their own is fine but if your team doesn't understand what the result needs to be the score will be irrelevant. Ideally you want to know what you're achieving now to determine your current results and then what your future results could be. Having big ambitious goals is fine for entrepreneurs, but for most people if they believe a goal is unrealistic they will never buy in to it and the process will fail.

Current

The next step is to try to determine what your current scores for each dial are. Can you trackback over a period of time to see what you've previously achieved for each of your three key performance indicators?

Again, don't be embarrassed if you don't know this information. If gathering this information would involve lots of work, just track your results for a month or two and then determine what the targets should be. Whatever you do please don't try to guess.

If you can easily see what your previous results were:

- Do the results fluctuate, i.e. is there any seasonality in your business?

- Are there any exceptional results you need to ignore to give you a realistic baseline?

Future

Based on the information gathered above and looking at your business goals we determined in Chapter One, what do your results need to be in each dial, each month? Look back at your Five-Year Success Plan. Within your numbers you should be able to break them down to yearly, weekly and daily targets.

For example, our three key performance indicators are: sales orders, jobs completed and revenue invoiced.

Sales Orders are determined by:

- The number of Leads that convert into Sales Orders

- Value of Sales Orders

Therefore, if we know 50% of Leads convert to Sales Orders and the average Order Value is £10,000, to achieve a monthly revenue of £100,000, you will need:

- 20 Leads

- 50% convert to Sales Order, average £10,000 each

- = 10 Sales & £100,000 Sales Revenue

If each Sales Order was one job you would need to complete 10 jobs per month and invoice them to achieve your monthly revenue target.

So your dashboard would look something like this:

Sample Dashboard

Sales This Month				Operations This Month		
	Target	Actual			Target	Actual
Leads	20	10		Jobs Completed	10	10
Orders	£100,000	£100,000		Invoiced	£100,000	£100,000

Of course, all months and weeks aren't created equal. I always work on a 50 week year to remove the two weeks in December which, for most businesses, are a washout. Most businesses have some fluctuations during a year in terms of achieving sales or getting orders processed. This is where your historic information comes into play. While you'll have a yearly target, you'll need to set monthly targets in line with your monthly variations. There's no point setting a target you have no chance of achieving.

Step Three: Record the score

For each dial on your dashboard you should now know:

1. How you're going to gather the information

2. What you're current performance is

3. The targets you're going to set each day and month

The next step is to determine how you're going to display this information. Again I've seen many Business Owners' eyes light up at this point when they start to Google 'business dashboards' and 'KPI software'. Don't be distracted, our rule here is: Keep It Simple. Let's focus on the outcome of what we're trying to achieve; we're looking to help the team pull together through a common goal and to get the business results focused.

Here's my suggestion for you to keep it simple and get this up and running within 48 hours.

1. Go onto Amazon (other retailers are available) to buy a dry marker board, around £25 with choice of pens, and thin black tape, around £5.

2. Once arrived screw it on a wall where everyone will see it daily.

3. Create a simple design, splitting your board into segments for each 'dial'. For each dial you need:

   - Month target & actual

   - Daily target & actual

   - Optional is yearly target & actual

4. Discuss with the team who is going to fill in each dial and hold them accountable to update their part of the board

The Magic Ingredient

I mentioned this above, **the process is as important as the result.**

"When you start to record this information, magic starts to happen…"

This magic happens for three reasons. One, by our very nature we humans are competitive. Two, we don't like failure. Three, we don't like letting others down.

Ideally the person responsible needs to update their dial. For example, the person who is responsible for generating sales revenue should update the sales revenue dial with the achievement each day. Here's why.

1. We're competitive and that person will want to improve or beat their score.

2. If they don't achieve the score they'll feel failure, failure equals pain and we don't like pain.

3. Accountability to the team, they know they need to do their bit and they won't want to let the team down.

There's no hiding from the focus of what's required. There's no hiding from what's been achieved. There's no hiding from what they need to do tomorrow.

Do the same for the person responsible for the other elements on your dashboard. If this has been done right you should now have a business focused on:

- What they need to achieve

- What they have achieved

- What they need to achieve tomorrow

In due course, automate this process by linking into your various systems. You might already have the ability to do this. I could tell you all about the flexibility of Google Sheets or some great dashboard software I've found and used. But, keep it simple and use the magic ingredient. I will challenge you to do it faster, for less cost and with more effect than a simple £25 wipe board.

Step Four: Share

Your final step of this process is to launch this to your team. Make sure you share with them the 'why'. Why you're doing it and what's in it for them. Don't be afraid to share the thinking behind what you're trying to achieve and how it fits with the vision and values of the business.

Explain the process of updating the dashboard and the meaning of the numbers it presents. Describe what it will mean for them, and the business, if they achieve the targets.

Don't be afraid to drill into people the actions each department needs to do to drive the results behind each dial. They need to know how what they do each day can affect the bigger result, but keep it simple.

Business Challenge

If you're feeling brave at this point you could offer up a challenge and reward scheme. Again it doesn't have to be over-complicated or costly, remember our rule here – keep it simple.

With many of my clients we use fish-n-chip or pizza Fridays. If we achieve this result or challenge, on the first Friday of the following month we'll order in lunch for everyone. With one of my clients, this has been so successful the team keep smashing their monthly targets (even when we increased them by over 20%) and every Friday they enjoy fish-n-chips.

We've also used team events, days out or just going out for a drink after work. The importance is to keep the momentum going and have some fun.

Control Summary

In this chapter we've now completed the four steps to enable you to build a dashboard for your business.

In step one we defined the company goals that will drive your business forward and towards your vision. Step two, we worked out how we're going to measure the goals. Step three, we built a dashboard to record your key goals. And in step four we launched and shared the goals and dashboard with all the team.

Everyone in your business should know if they've done a good job that day. At the end of each working day they should be able to reflect and know if they achieved what was expected of them. Ideally, when they leave that day their line manager or a screen on a wall should be able to tell them if they have achieved the score they were expecting.

If we go back to Herzberg's Two-Factor Theory, one of the key motivation factors is achievement; people are motivated by achievement. I'm sure you can remember a reward chart at home or school when we were very young and that magical feeling of achievement we got when another sticker or tick went on the chart. It's no different for adults, we're all motivated by achievement and teams are united through a common aim or purpose.

And it's no different for you. Again one of the reasons you've fallen out of love with your business is you've lost your sense of achievement. You've got dragged into a rut of trying to cope with the day-to-day and lost sight of what you want to achieve and knowing where you are on the journey. That, in turn, makes the journey feel like a constant traffic jam. It goes back to one of our core principles, **the journey is more important than the destination**. You've got to enjoy the journey.

Enjoyment comes from having fun doing what you do and the sense of achievement you get from it.

Without a dashboard in your business, in effect you're getting into your car every day without knowing how fast you're going or how far along the journey you are.

And it's the same for your team, they don't know what's expected of them and what the score is.

CASH

"Never take your eyes off the cash flow, it's the life blood of business."

Sir Richard Branson

"If we keep focused on increasing our sales revenue we'll make more money...won't we?"

Without a doubt this is the single biggest reason most entrepreneurs fall out of love with their business. They get sucked into the myth that big is beautiful and that big companies make more money. This couldn't be any further from the truth. What ends up happening is that business owners work harder and harder, the business works harder and harder, and they increase their revenue. Six to nine months after year-end their accountant tells them their profits aren't high enough to cover their dividends.

"The harder I work the less money I earn."

The business owner feels quite dejected after working their butt off the previous year to have less money in their pocket.

But I understand how difficult it is for you to know what good looks like. The vast majority of businesses like yours only have to submit abbreviated accounts to Companies House and this creates an effect of 'smoke and mirrors' behind what's really going on with company finances. Their turnover and profits are hidden and without analysing their balance sheets it's not easy to see what's going on in the business. It's therefore difficult for you to benchmark your business and know if your results are better or worse. And with a bit of ego, bravado and the odd credit card or two, it's easy for others to appear to be living the dream when you're not.

This is made worse when companies like 'Plimsoll' send you a summary report about how you're faring in your industry. They'll tell you the net profits and the average turnover of companies in your sector. But how can they? If they get the information from Companies House these are predominately on abbreviated accounts and therefore you probably need to take these reports with a pinch of salt.

Because of my role with businesses I get to see many actual detailed accounts. At times it can be quite shocking how little some companies, and, in turn, the owners, earn each year. Some business owners would be better off getting a job and working on minimum wage, especially given the stress and hours they work. But they plough on believing it will all come good if they carry on doing what they've always done. Come on, that's not the lifestyle you really wanted when you started on this journey. What's our number one principle? The journey is more important than the destination.

Where does it go wrong for you?

There's a high chance that you're technically very sound at what you do. You'll have a deep passion for the stuff your business does for your customers. Very rarely will those talents extend to a deep understanding and ability to manage the finances of a £1m-plus company. It's not your expertise or passion. What you need is the support of a financial director but taking on that cost is not viable.

What can you do?

You need to get focused on the numbers.

Predominantly, profitable businesses fail because they run out of cash. This is notorious in high growth businesses; they grow and grow but lose sight of generating cash.

Remember the urban business saying:

"Turnover is vanity, profit is sanity and cash is reality" This isn't quite true. Why?

Because business owners wrongly believe this means the business bank account and they run the business based on what's in the bank.

And that brings us on to How To Fall Back In Love With Your Business, principle four:

Your primary goal must focus on generating real cash.

And real cash comes from cashflow.

Your biggest challenge, and the greatest challenge for most businesses, is managing cashflow; struggling month to month balancing the money in and out of their bank account. This is particularly difficult for companies that are achieving high growth. You must invest to grow. The business needs to buy something before they get paid. Invariably you'll buy materials, parts or labour upfront. If you're working with corporate customers you might be on 60, 90 or 120 day payment terms. If you're buying stock, you're most likely paying for it before you've sold it and getting paid by your customers.

Here's a real life example.

I worked on a business growth project with an engineering business which supplied specialist services to high-end manufacturing plants. I worked with the client to win a £1m-plus contract to fit out a new factory with a six to eight month completion target. At first he was unbelievably excited about how this project was going to enable his business to grow and make him a good margin. "It's going to enable us to have a smashing year, Adrian."

That was until I gave him a sense of reality.

During the scoping stage of the project, I looked at how the payment process was going to work, and it worked out you got paid 60 days after sign-off at various phases during construction.

"Paul, how quickly do you think you'll be able to complete each one of these phases", I asked.

"Probably every six to eight weeks" came the reply.

"Okay, in that case you're going to need about £480,000 to fund this project" I stated.

"What do you mean?"

"To run this project you'll need about £480,000 of cash to fund your work in progress, before you get paid you will need to spend £480,000 to buy materials and pay your guys."

As you can imagine, the colour drained from his face and his jaw dropped to the floor. After a few expletives aimed at me, he calmed and replied, "Okay, explain how you've worked that out."

I drew Paul a timeline showing the 26 weeks of the £1m project. "Your normal labour to materials rate is about 66% labour and 34% materials. Therefore during the project you'll burn £25,000 a week in labour. Between each sign-off phase, roughly seven weeks, you'll spend £175,000 on labour plus the eight weeks you'll have to wait to get paid, which is another £200,000. In total £375,000 for labour (his guys were paid weekly.). We need to add material costs. This is roughly £13,000 per week. We can probably negotiate 60 day terms, but it will still mean you won't get paid for around eight weeks after you've paid your suppliers. So we need to add £13,000 times 8 = £104,000. In total, you'll need around £480,000. Yes these figures at your charge out rate, not your cost, but that will give us a bit of 'fat' for any slippage in time or costs, or delays in payments. This also needs to be on top of your normal working cash flow."

"Holy shit" exclaimed Paul.

From this example you can see how easy it is to get into deep financial problems when you win these large projects. It's no wonder why so many small contractors go bankrupt. It would have been very easy to brush over the financial burden of this project and wonder why the business went bankrupt. The profit margin was good for the project, but as I've already stated, it's not uncommon to find profitable companies going pop.

Fortunately, Paul had a very good relationship with this customer, and his customer really wanted his company to do the job. We prepared a cash flow statement for the project which Paul presented to them. They agreed to pre-pay for materials and shorter four-week project sign-off phases paid within 30 days, so we managed to negotiate the required funding from £480,000 down to around £200,000.

Your primary goal must focus on generating real cash.

To fall back in love with your business you're going to need to get close to your numbers. The good news is I've got a proven approach which will enable you to make and get control of your cash.

There are four critical elements to making cash and I call them CASH:

1. C = Costs

2. A = Assets

3. S = Sales

4. H = HMRC

I'll go through each one of these in turn and give you practical advice and a process for managing them. I'll try to keep it as simple as possible and I'll apologise now to any accountants who may disagree with some of my terminologies, but I'm sure they'll agree with the approach. I'll also apologise if at times I'm teaching you 'how to suck eggs' as I explain some of the accounting terms and principles. In my experience, I've found wide differences in accounting knowledge with business owners and I think it's better to ensure there is the base understanding. You can always speed-read these bits.

If you go to www.betterneverstops.global/tools you'll find a working template to assist you with this chapter.

Costs

We'll start first with COSTS. Within my model there are two elements to costs:

1. Cost of Goods Sold (COGS) or Cost of Sales (COS), they both mean the same thing. These are all costs directly associated with your sales revenue. For example the products or materials you purchase which you resell to your customers.

2. Overheads or expenses, again both mean the same thing. These are the costs you incur to run your business but which cannot be directly attributed to a single customer. Costs such as heating, light, marketing, electric, phones etc.

There's another way of thinking about the difference between the two above.

Cost of Goods Sold – Costs in your business which are directly attributed to each customer invoice. These costs would rise and fall with each customer transaction.

Overheads – each month, expenses your business incur even if it didn't raise a single customer invoice. These costs are in your business whether you have customers or not. These are sometimes referred to as your fixed costs.

The only exception to the above is employment costs. These should ideally be split out to show:

▪ Labour costs that are directly attributed to Cost of Goods Sold, for example, your factory workers or installers or engineers. Their time and costs can easily be attributed to a single sales invoice.

- Office or administration or directors should be shown under Overheads. These employment costs are absorbed into running the business.

But in my experience these are rarely shown this way, most accounts present all employment costs under Overheads. This has the effect of distorting your Gross Profit result:

Sales Revenue minus COGS (parts, materials, shipping, commissions) = Gross Profit.

This isn't a disaster but as your business grows you'll want to see your overheads remain relatively fixed as sales revenue increases, and thus you make more overall or net profit:

Sales Revenue minus COGS minus Overheads = Net Profit.

This becomes difficult to see if your direct labour costs are lumped into your overheads.

Managing Overheads

Our first action under Costs is to focus in on your Overhead costs. This is where you'll get more 'bangs for your bucks.' Some business owners focus on generating more revenue or increasing profits and ignore overhead costs. Here's a very good reason why we start with managing overhead cost.

If you make 50% gross profit per sale, £1 saved on overheads is worth a £2 increase in sales revenue. If you make 33% gross profit, £1 saved is worth £3 in sales revenue.

Let me explain how this works:

Let's say you saved £50,000 in overhead costs and you make 50% gross profit; one, that's an instant £50,000 of net profit you'll make and two, you would need an extra £100,000 in revenue to get the same result by increasing sales.

If you make 33% gross profit it's worth an extra £150,000 increase in sales. Overnight I'm not sure there's many businesses that can make that change to their sales revenues.

Overheads Review

When was the last time you or someone in your team went through all your overhead expenses line by line? If you don't already, you need to create an annual budget to manage and track these costs on a monthly basis. Again you'll find a template in our tools sections on our website; www.BetterNeverStops.Global/Tools and look for CASH Review.

Step 1: Get a live expense report from your accounts system. This should be a list of all your costs for the last twelve months.

Step 2: Go to the Overhead Budget Tab in the CASH Review Template

Step 3: For each cost item in your accounts report enter the item name and the current annual cost. The sheet will automatically divide and put this into a monthly cost. Once all the costs are itemised here's your challenge: in the row 'Totals' you'll see your annual overhead costs. How much can you save? Set yourself a goal.

Step 4: Work with your team to find ways to reduce each overhead cost and under the 'Reviewed' column mark as:

Same – it will stay the same over the next year

Lower – you've managed to reduce the cost for the year

Higher – during the year you're going to see an increase

Step 5: Put the revised cost into column 'New Year Cost', again this will automatically be broken into a monthly cost.

Step 6: This information is now saved in the Monthly Budget sheet and each month you can review your overhead costs against your budget. Here you'll be able to track variances from the budget and investigate why.

Increasing Gross Profit

The next step under COSTS is to look at your Cost of Goods Sold. In the same way you reviewed your Overheads, you need to look at the costs you incur while making or delivering your services for your customers. When was the last time you negotiated terms with your suppliers? This will vary greatly from industry to industry but within our CASH Review template you'll see a tracker to manage COGS. Here's a few things you need to think about in this section:

- Speak to your main suppliers about creating stronger partnerships.

  - Negotiate with them to improve terms for price and payments. If you pay faster will they give you extra discounts? If you can't reduce prices, can you get other benefits, like free or reduced-rate shipping?

- By working together are there ways you can take cost and time out of the process?

- If you know your expected volumes over a period of time, can you bulk purchase products to reduce cost?

- Are there opportunities to improve products or services offered to create lower cost and premium products?

- If the service you receive from the supplier is not the best, can you work together to improve it, or find another supplier?

■ Review your production process. Could you use less expensive materials without reducing the quality of your overall product?

■ Can you reduce waste in your manufacturing and in the supply process?

■ Can you join forces with others in your industry or your customers, to form buying groups to reduce costs?

Using the template update the budget to track and manage Gross Profit.

Assets

We now move onto your Assets and under this section there are four key areas we're going to look at:

1. Stock

2. Work In Progress

3. Creditors – people you owe money to

4. Debtors – people who owe you money

These four items sit on your balance sheet and from my experience these are seldom looked at by business owners. If you keep on top of these through good housekeeping, there's some 'real gold hidden in here' in terms of unrequired stress and extra cash.

1. Stock - when was the last time you reviewed your stock levels?

    -   Are you carrying redundant stock? Have a full stock review to find old stock items or very slow movers. These items have been paid for and by selling these off you'll generate cash into your bank. It may be you'll need to just dispose of non-sellable items or receive scrap money for them. If nothing else just think of the space you'll create.

    -   Are you carrying too much stock and in turn have cash tied up in your stock? Another way to improve your cash flow is to carry less stock. There is sometimes a careful balance between getting good terms with your suppliers and buying in bulk. But commit to reviewing how quickly you turn over your stock. Toyota famously uses the 'Just In Time' principle (JIT), this is where suppliers ship small batches of products just as they need them thus reducing stock and increasing cash flow. How could you use this in your business?

2. Work In Progress – this refers to the time it takes you to turn sales orders into sales invoices, which ties cash up in the form of stock and labour because you'll most likely pay for these before getting paid. This is only really applicable to companies whose Sales Order to Sales Invoice time is over 30 days. We'll cover this in more depth in the next chapter, Efficiency, when we look at reducing process complexity and increasing speed. Here we'll just focus on the need to speed up the Work In Progress time to get you paid faster.

When working with an Electrical Contracting company, I sat with the owner and the accounts team reviewing their CASH. We discovered they only invoiced every couple of weeks, and worst still, if someone was on holiday it could go down to once a month. When I asked the accounts team why they invoiced this way, they replied "Because we've always done it this way."

Not surprisingly this was easy to resolve and we very quickly fixed it. But my message here for you is: don't be afraid to ask the simple questions, assume nothing.

What stops you getting paid when you take a sales order?

Are there simple ways you can increase the speed of delivery to get products invoiced quickly? Who's responsible for invoicing and are they getting orders invoiced without delay?

Could you take deposits or staged payments? A similar approach is to reduce the size of projects or break them into smaller steps.

3. Creditors – these are your suppliers to whom you owe money. Hard nosed finance managers would have you pushing terms as far as possible. Aggressive large corporate companies force their suppliers to accept 120 day or more payment terms. But given half a chance, their suppliers would stop working with them. In small business land, I'm a firm believer in working in partnership with suppliers for the good of everyone, a "do as you would be done by" approach.

Decrease the number of key suppliers so you can work closer with them. Have review meetings with them to discuss:

- Improving discounts and payment terms

- Reviewing working process to reduce complexity and waste

- Investigating ways to reduce material storage and transportation costs

- Looking at opportunities to share product development and improvements

- Can you combine forces to increase buying power?

4. Debtors, these are the customers who you provide credit to. This is often a difficult or sensitive subject as most businesses I work with are in very competitive environments. There's often a feeling that you must be super cautious around customers when discussing getting paid.

"We'll just use someone else" is a classic bully tactic used by customers. But don't get sucked into this trap.

Customers who don't pay you are poor customers, period.

If customers want extended payment terms build it into the price, but they want 'cheap', you should also get quick. It's not until you sit and analyse customers that you realise the time taken in administration can far outweigh the profit you make on that customer.

Using your accounting software and by working with your accounts/admin team, put together a list of customers and their average payment times.

Who is always a difficult payer?

- Try to have a meeting with them to discuss how you can work together to improve processes, reduce costs and resolve issues with payments

- For notorious poor payers increase their prices to balance the time and extra resource it takes to get paid. They'll either pay it or go somewhere else, both results are good.

- Put all customers onto direct debit payments. If they have payment terms, i.e. 30 days from the invoice date, the money is directly debited from their accounts in 30 days. In effect, this saves them time in scheduling payments via their banks. This sounds slightly scary at first but it's standard practice with many large companies like utilities and mobile phones. Many direct debit providers like GoCardless and EasyCollect handle the compliance and process relativity cheaply and hassle-free. If a customer doesn't want to go on Direct Debit they are basically saying "we don't want to pay you on time", so reduce their terms. Remember, customers who don't pay you are poor customers and you don't want them.

Sales

Let's look now at our fourth CASH step, Sales. There are four (and only four) elements that drive sales:

1. The number of Leads, that is, the volume and quality of people who raise their hand to say "I'm interested in buying your product".

2. Sales Conversion, the number of Leads you turn into orders.

3. The Sales Order value, the price you charge and any add-ons you generate.

4. Repeat sales, the number of times you sell to that customer.

We'll cover the strategies for these in much more depth in our chapter Scale, but they fit here because they'll be some simple and quick wins which can have an immediate effect on CASH in your business.

These Sales steps will be really powerful if you implement more than one because they have a multiplying effect on your revenue. Let me explain:

Current			Increase each element by 10%	
Leads		100		110
Sales Conversion	@ 50%	50	@ 55%	60
Order Value	@ £1,000	£50,000	@ £1,100	£66,550
Repeat Orders	@ 10	£500,000	@ 11	£732.050
Total		£550,000		£798,600

Increase = £248,600. The increase isn't 10%, it's a 45% increase.

Yes this example is simplistic and you may feel it's unrealistic but I can assure you it works. I've used and implemented these principles in many businesses and, when brought together, the results each time have been outstanding. You can see how if you make little tweaks in your sales they multiply the outcome through the process. It might be you can't get 10% on each element, you might be able to increase leads by 5% and something else by 7% but the multiply effect still happens, just at a different rate.

How can you increase each element?

Leads

Talk to you team about your current marketing efforts:

- How many leads is the business currently generating per day/week/month?

- How are the leads currently coming into your business?

- Which lead generation strategies are having the best results?

- Can you increase the amount of activity or spend in this area to generate more?

- Is the quality of the leads good, i.e. are these the right target market for you?

- If not, why not and how can you 'fish' in the right pond to attract the right leads?

Sales Conversions

How do you measure sales conversion?

Let's get something cleared up as this tends to tie many businesses up in knots.

There are many ways to calculate sales conversion rates. Here is the simplest, most effective and accurate.

1. Agree with your sales team how long the typical sales process is, i.e. from when a customer first makes contact to when they buy. This is important as I've seen Leads carried over for months and months without being closed off. These

are never going to convert so they should be closed as lost and not left as 'pending' or 'open'.

2. Leads should only have three categorises; New, Won and Lost.

3. When a Lead is Won or Lost you mark it appropriately recording the date and if Lost, the reason why.

4. When a Lead reaches the end of the agreed sales process time period they are closed as Lost, the closed date and the reason recorded against them.

5. Each month you measure the number of Leads Won & Lost based on the date the Lead was closed (Won or Lost); divide the number of Won against the Total Leads Won and Lost for the closed Leads that month and here's your conversion rate. Won 10, Lost 5, Total = 15, 10 divided by 15 (x100) = 66.7%

If your typical sales process takes more than one month, you'll have a rolling conversion rate. This might take a bit of a hit as you close old Leads but it will soon resemble something more accurate.

Don't get bamboozled into:

-   Worrying about when the Lead was generated, with a constant flow of Leads it actually doesn't matter.

-   Having a 'pending' status. The sales period is the sales period and it's either Won or Lost. For any Lost that later convert (which are normally quite rare) reopen the Lead and change the outcome and date.

Trust this approach, I have implemented this across many clients and it is the   only way to remove 'sales wish lists'; these are lists of Leads hoarded in a   false belief that at some point they will convert. They don't, so get focused on true sales conversion.

We've got that tidied up and you've now got a reasonable handle on your sales conversion rate.

- What are the reasons why these Leads don't convert?

- Hand on heart, are your leads followed up in a timely and systemised way?

- If not, when did you last review the sales process to increase the quality and frequency of sales follow-ups? **The fortune is in the follow-up.** Many companies stop following up way too quickly because we're too nice. "We don't want to be a pain". Here's a simple trick: get permission to recontact at each contact stage process stage by asking the Lead "When would be a good time to contact you again?" When you recontact you can begin with "Hi John, I'm just calling you as promised three days ago…"

- Are you using good quality sales materials within your sales process, i.e. do you have a nice brochure or quote pack which presents your products and services and explains the benefits of what you do?

Sales Revenue

- When was the last time you reviewed your prices? Over the last few years your costs will have risen quite considerably and without realising it this will have had a dramatic effect on profits. Now I know what you're thinking, the very thought of increasing your prices is making your toes curl: "my customers will never agree to that." There are four certainties in life: death, taxes, change and customers moaning about prices. We conduct numerous customer research and satisfaction surveys, customers will score you 10 out of 10 for services, quality of product etc etc, but when asked what you could improve, most reply price. Don't be put off by this. In my experience most don't even notice a 10-15% rise. In most cases you haven't even got to tell them unless you're on agreed price lists or contract. In some industries they have an ongoing annual, six monthly or quarterly price increase.

- Enforce your terms of trade. I've come across many clients who have trading terms but don't enforce them, i.e. "the price is based on a minimum order quantity of 500, if an order is less we reserve the right to increase unit cost to x". Many are reluctant to use it but when they have customers haven't stopped using them. In some cases they've increased the quantities of orders, "Oh, I didn't realise, can we increase order to x."

- Speak to your team about how you could add more value to your products without adding more cost.

    - Ask your customers "how else could we help you today?"

- What other products could you add to an order to enhance the sale?

Repeat Sales

- How many times do your current customers come back to you?

- What types of customers are most likely to come back over a period?

- Within your lead generation how can you increase the number of these types of customers?

- Are there any ways you could increase the frequency of purchase, by adding other products or by adding a loyalty scheme?

HMRC

Our last CASH step is HMRC, yes, our friends at HM Revenue and Customs. There are five key elements to this step:

1. Corporation Tax, making sure the business is claiming all the allowances it's entitled to.

2. VAT, keeping good records and putting aside money each month to pay the VAT liability.

3. PAYE, making sure you're claiming all the benefit in kind allowances.

4. Personal Tax, making sure your relationship with the business is tax efficient.

5. Grants, central and local government schemes to help growing businesses.

We'll go through each one of these in turn, but I want to make it clear that I'm not a tax expert. Any 'tax benefits' I suggest below need to be discussed with your accountant because they aren't necessarily right for all business owners and allowances and benefits can change. The items I'm going to discuss below need to act like a discussion list for you.

If you make a profit you're going to pay tax, remember the four certainties in life; Death, Tax, Change and Prices. I'm afraid it's going to happen. But remember my job here is to enable you to fall back in love with your business. Two of your major frustrations will involve managing cash flow and how much you earn, both of which we're going to tackle here.

Corporation Tax

There are two key elements to managing your Corporation Tax:

1. Allowances – Making sure the business is claiming all the allowances it's entitled to.

2. Liability – Putting aside monies to pay your corporation tax liability so that when needed it's already in a bank account.

1. Allowances

At the time of writing UK corporation tax is set at 19%, therefore you'll pay 19% of your net profits to HMRC (for every £100 of net profit you'll pay £19). But there are legal and approved schemes to lower your profits and therefore reduce your corporation tax payment. Rarely do I find companies making best use of these schemes which can be significantly advantageous.

1. Research and Development Tax Credits (R&D Tax Credits)

If your company invests time, resource and expenses to improving systems, working methods or the development of products/services, you can claim these development costs at an enhanced rate, currently 230%. In very simple terms this is how it works, but you'll need to work with a R&D Tax specialist to implement.

- You get your R&D project approved by HMRC.

- You track your time and expenses spent on the project(s).

- At year end, all these are totalled up and deducted from your net profits @ 230%. i.e. if you've spent £10,000 on R&D approved projects, you can reduce your corporation tax liability by a further £13,000 (£10,000 will have already been in your costs).

- As I understand it, R&D can be claimed back for up to 3 years and can also be rolled forward towards future profits.

2. Relevant Life Insurance

Do you pay for your life insurance personally, i.e. out of your own bank account?

If yes, you need to consider a Relevant Life Insurance policy. The cover and cost work pretty much the same as your current personal life policy. The difference is that the company pays for the cover rather than you. In effect when you pay your life insurance, you've already paid tax and National Insurance on the money. With Relevant Life, it's a cost to the business and therefore reduces the net profit. And here's the great news, there's no Benefit-In-Kind to you, i.e. you don't pay tax or National Insurance as a taxable benefit. Another nice part to it, this can be extended to other key members of your team or even the whole team. I've got clients who have rolled this out to everyone within a pay rise or as a bonus. You'll need to speak to your Financial Adviser or search 'Relevant Life' for more information.

3. Company Pension Schemes For Directors
    As a company director you can extract profits from your business into tax efficient pension schemes. These are a great way to reduce company profits as pension payments are a cost to the business and if they are paid right, can qualify for personal income tax relief.

    There are also certain pension schemes that allow you to use part of your funds to invest in company assets via loans.

    Again, this is not my field of expertise, but I want to get this on your radar and for you to seek specialist advice from a Financial Advisor.

2. Liability – Putting aside monies to pay your corporation tax liability.

If you're making a profit you're going to pay tax. As your business grows these payments and liabilities have a habit of creeping up on you. They create a heap of added, unwanted stress and pressure on you, and your cashflow. Most businesses leave paying the corporation tax to as late as possible to avoid the fine.

Without trying to sound like your mum, you knew about this liability long before it was due, so it is avoidable.

Here's what I advise all my clients to do and it's pretty simple:

1. At the beginning of each year work out how much you're likely to pay in Corporation Tax. You could just use the previous year to start with. Or you can work with your accountant to fine tune it. Put this into your monthly cashflow budget (we'll be going through an example at the end of this chapter).

2. Each month either put the money aside into a separate business account or pay to HMRC. Any prepayments you make, the HMRC will pay you interest on. The intention is that by the time you need to pay your Corporation Tax bill, you've got all or most of the funds in a separate account or already deposited with the HMRC. Work on a plan so that each month you'll know roughly how much it's likely to be and take the amount from your day-to-day bank account. It's very likely with the HMRC's Making Tax Digital programme that the timeframes and the process for paying Corporation Tax will change significantly and the money will be directly taken from your account in the same way as VAT.

VAT

Which brings us nicely onto VAT. This step is very simple:

1. Make sure you keep good records and they are up to date.

2. At the end of each month, work out your VAT in and VAT out, the difference between the two becomes your VAT liability. All accounting software will allow you to run a report to show this. Move this amount to another account ready for when your payment is due. No nasty surprises or scabbing around trying to balance your cashflow.

Employees

Like corporation tax there are various allowances you can claim for staff without paying Benefit-In-Kind. Again these change from time to time but currently here's some ideas:

- Salary sacrifice schemes

- Cycle to work scheme

- Child care

- Work wear

- Employee suggestion schemes

- Tax free loans

- Functions & parties – £150 per head

- Professional Membership Fees

Your Personal Tax

Although the UK Government seems to be hell bent on removing benefits for business owners, there are still ways to minimise your tax and National Insurance payments. The most beneficial structure still appears to be a company director taking a small salary and dividends. You can claim the same benefits as above and there also other tax efficient allowances you can claim:

- £300 per year in 'Trival' Benefits

- School Fees

- Home Office

- Business Mileage

All of the above are just suggestions of benefits you may get, for up to date information speak to your accountant and/or a tax advisor.

Grants

The final part under HMRC is Grants. This could be a chapter in its own right, but the challenge is that as fast as I could write it, it would be out of date.

But what I do is share my experience of using Grants in your business and some hows to get started.

First of all, why would you want them?

How would you like some free money? "But it's never free, Adrian." In this case it is. The Government has a policy to re-invest in the UK economy. In a very simplistic way, if it helps businesses to grow, develop new products and create wealth and employment; it creates more HMRC income via taxes and increases Gross Domestic Product, hence the Government's motivation.

There are many grant schemes mostly delivered at regional or county level. I've seen grants as high as 50% but typically, they are normally around 20-25%. And typically they are capped at £25k, £100k or £500k in terms of full project cost. One of my clients had a significant extension to his building and claimed back around £30,000.

What's The Catch?

There isn't one really. Obviously you have to spend the money, and whatever you do, don't spend anything until it's approved. Some are only provided on a 'new employee' per grant amount basis. There are some caveats and restrictions but the principle is the same and worth investigating to help your business expansion.

My only words of warning…

Some of the grant applications can be time consuming. From experience, if your grant isn't for more than £5,000, sometimes the time you'll invest in the application process will outweigh any benefit. Also, the speed in which the grants can be awarded aren't always fast enough.

To find out more about grants in your area search for 'business grants in <your county>'. This should find your Local Enterprise

Partnership (LEP) provider. They are normally helpful and will provide free telephone or face-to-face grant advice.

CASH Summary

In this chapter we've focused on how you can fall back in love with your business by getting close to your numbers. This is based on our fourth principle;

Your primary goal must focus on generating real cash.

Real cash comes from cashflow and through the chapter I've detailed my CASH model I use with my clients. By using this model and the tools you can significantly improve the cash position of your business by:

- Getting better control of your COSTS

- Using your ASSETS smarter

- Finding quick wins to generate more SALES

- Working within the rules of HMRC to claim and manage tax liabilities

Your action now is to apply this model to your business using the knowledge above and the tools provided on our website, www.betterneverstops.global/tools.

Trust me, if you focus on the above and manage your cashflow, you will significantly reduce the monthly 'have we got enough money in the bank' stress. The business will be easier to run and you'll increase your personal wealth.

But, it will take time and patience to slowly build your reserves and put your business into a strong cash position.

If you need any further help, work with your accountant to get the support you need and build a close relationship with them. Good accountants love getting into this level of detail, it's what they thrive on and how they add proper value. My own accountant, Jason, is a great guy and I've referred him into many of my clients because he loves this type of work.

If this is not your accountant, or you feel you couldn't have this type of relationship with them, don't be afraid to change accountants, maybe you've outgrown them. There's not a shortage of good accountants and a change will do you good.

Also you need to find yourself a good, trusted Financial Advisor. The good ones are worth their salt, and working with your accountant will show you a proven path to working your profits tax efficiently and to build your wealth.

EFFICIENCY

"It is not the most intellectual of the species that survives; it is not the strongest that survives; but the one that is most responsive to change."

Charles Darwin Origin of Species

I love this quote by Charles Darwin because it's also so true for businesses. Just look at the last ten years and the number of brands that have disappeared because they didn't change and evolve to their environment or market place. And these weren't small companies; Comet, BHS, C&A, Woolworths, Blockbuster, Austin Reed, Staples, Maplin and Toys'R'Us, at their peak were all £100m-plus per year companies.

And I see this so much in small businesses. They get stuck in the "but we've always done it this way" syndrome, particularly when it comes to their business processes.

As businesses grow they can become fat and lazy. In the beginning, they were slick and lean, the business owner was at the heart of everything. But as the business grows, more people get involved in the processes, bad habits form with poor disciplines and over-complexity. There's a strong belief that the only way to improve is to throw more staff at it.

This leads to increased overhead costs, poor customer experience and frustration for all staff. The Business Owner gets really frustrated: "ahhhhh, business used to be so much easier."

The challenge for you as the business owner is that you're a control freak and a perfectionist. Yep, sorry, unfortunately it's a by-product of being an entrepreneur and here's why:

- You're really, really passionate about what you do.

- You also care about the services you provide for your customers.

- You believe everything you do should be top quality because it has your name on it.

- There's many jobs you believe only you can do in your business and you don't trust others to do them.

Do some of these sound familiar? The mindset you have has got you a long way and to where you are today. Getting your business over £1m in turnover and employing more than three people puts you in the top percentile of business.

But I'm here to enable you to fall back in love with your business. One of your major frustrations is:

"The harder I work, the less money I make."

The mindset and approach which got you here was great, but to grow beyond it something has to change. I want you to rekindle that entrepreneur's mindset and, as we've already discussed in this book, you need to start looking at your business in a different way.

Many business owners spend lots of time trying to save money, entrepreneurs spend money to save time.

There's a big difference.

Many modern day wizz kids have used technology to solve a problem for themselves, and this ends us being so great others want to buy it. They monetise it and boom, they have a million-plus business.

Technology can play and should play a big part in your business. So much more can be achieved for less cost by using technology and automation. Your customers will increasingly be wanting more, faster and with less complexity. Retail shopping habits are increasingly crossing over into our business buying habits. Businesses are getting more and more comfortable and confident about buying services and products online or with reduced complexity. You've got to change with the times. Only three things in life are guaranteed, death, taxes and CHANGE. Through technology the world has got significantly smaller and that rate of change seems faster than ever.

The good news

There is a better way. But, it's going to take a lot of courage and time. I know you haven't got any extra time, you're far too busy.

But I'll give you a really strong reason why you should…

Because if you don't your competitors will, and you'll get left behind, and at a great rate of speed.

In this chapter I'll take you through how we enabled businesses to take hours out of their processes, saving time, cost and improving the service delivered to customers.

As you'd expect from me by now, there's a simple four step process to follow:

1. Map your current processes

2. Review

3. Map New and Add Technology

4. Test & Implement

A Lesson From Formula One

I'm a bit of a petrol head. I've been around cars and racing from a young age. When I was about 13 years old I started racing 100cc National Karts, I progressed onto F1 stock cars and finally to National Superstoxs. I've also watch Formula One racing on the TV from a young age, I've been a fan of Ayrton Senna, Nigel Mansell and Frank Williams having grown up with them and I've read their books.

Formula One is a harsh sport, it doesn't take any prisoners. You must be able to constantly adapt, change and improve. You can argue that "it's OK for them, they have multi-million-pound budgets, they can afford to." But they also must keep evolving their business model. And not just the teams, but the actual sport itself.

I constantly use Formula One as an analogy for how a business should think about change and improvement.

The car going around the track is your customer. Your customer wants faster, slicker and more efficient. If you don't improve your competitors will get ahead of you and if you do nothing you'll simply get left behind.

In today's F1 the time taken on a pitstop can win or lose a race. If you hop on my website I've two great videos showing the progress of pitstops.

1950 – shows a car coming in, two guys working on it with just one changing the tyres with a hammer to release the central wheel nut. Surprisingly they get it done in 50 seconds.

2013 – is what you'd expect in the modern day, and of course they get it done in less than two seconds.

In fact as I write this book, the Red Bull Team have just broken the world record at Silverstone with a time of 1.91 seconds.

My point is that your business needs to have the F1 mindset and be constantly thinking:

How can we be faster, slicker and more efficient?

Let's get cracking…

Map Current

You're going to need to set yourself time aside to do this exercise. There's a good chance you'll try to put this off for as long as possible because potentially it's going to be hard work and time consuming. To improve you need to know where you are and I promise you the business will eventually thank you for it.

There are two key rules to this process:

1. Reality is king – it's not what you think the process is, it's what actually happens day-to-day.

2. Don't try to fix it – while reviewing the processes it's tempting to dive in and start fixing. DON'T. You'll only slow the flow of review and lose sight of the purpose

What we want to achieve is to have all the business processes laid out on a floor, laid out on a table or hung up around a room. This way you can stand back and see the whole picture. It's also important to collect the paperwork or screen shots of the information and data you're collecting and inputting. This way you'll see process and underneath it the corresponding paperwork trail.

Start at the beginning of your customer's journey and work along until the final process, in most cases this is normally in accounts with the transaction getting reconciled with the bank.

At various points your customer passes through different departments or people. Here's how rule one above applies, you must get someone from that department to tell you how they do it. Remember Reality is King. You'll need to explain that the process isn't designed to catch anyone out, you're there to make the customer journey better. In order to do so you need to know what actually happens, not what people think happens.

Start at the beginning of your customers' journey. You'll need to work with marketing or sales. How does your customer first contact you? It will probably be in many ways: a contact form on your website, an email, a phone call. What information is collected, on what forms? Keep going through the process; what happens next? And next? Make sure the people doing the process are the ones telling you what happens. Keep collecting the paperwork including brochures and sales materials. What about suppliers' forms, how do they require information and in what form?

In some businesses this might be fairly straightforward, some will need a lot of room. Once you've got right the way through to the end of the customer journey, normally reconciling the bank account, stand back and look. This bit is normally the amazing "oh shit how did that happen?" moment when you realise the complexity of what you do.

Review

Every business tells me "But this is our industry Adrian", and "Our industry is different Adrian." Every business is different but the race is the same; you need to get your car around that track as fast, as slick and as efficiently as possible without crashing.

How complex is your customers' journey? How long does it take from a customer's point of view? How long does it take from a business point of view? How much physical time is spent processing the order?

Time = Cost; if you reduce time, you can reduce cost or increase ability to process more orders in less time. It's that simple.

When you stand back and start to review your customers' journey, think of it as a lap. I want you to take the F1 approach. How do we take time out of the lap?

Things to look for:

- How many times do you collect and rewrite the customer's details?

- What other information is duplicated along the route?

- Where are the bottlenecks, the places the process gets snarled up, and why?

- Are there places where it's most likely that there will be customer or quality issues?

- What steps in the process are customer critical points? For example communication points.

I want you to look at every process step or piece of paperwork or screen with the clear objective of removing it. The only reason it will stay is because it is either:

- Business Critical – without it we couldn't process a sales order or we have to collect for tax or compliance reasons.

- Customer Value – Our customer requires it and it adds value.

To help you decide which can stay I'll share with you our simple "Critical Value Window". The template can found on www.betterneverstops.global/tools.

Below is a sample of what it looks like.

I want you to be really harsh with your processes and each one needs to fall into a segment within the window below. Each process step is either:

Business Critical – you need to carry out this step or record this information because it's critical to enable the business to process the order or for compliance

Customer Value – you need to carry out this step or record this information because its value to your process

Not Critical – this is something you do because...? If it's something you do for the business but it's not critical it goes in here.

No Value - it's something you do for the customer but it doesn't add value and the customer wouldn't notice or care if you didn't do it.

CRITICAL VALUE WINDOW

BUSINESS CRITICAL	CUSTOMER VALUE
NOT CRITICAL	NO VALUE

Anything in the top sections needs to stay, but does it? Be ruthless with your processes and paperwork, if it doesn't add value or isn't critical, do you need it?

Anything in the bottom sections can go.

Map New

It's time to re-map your customers' journey. The objective is to take as many steps out of the process as possible. Steps are the bends on your race track, they're going to slow you down. The fastest form of racing is a drag strip, a straight line with no bends. Unfortunately it's unlikely your business could only have two processes, a start and a finish. But you want to have the least number of bends possible. Using your analysis from above and the Critical Value Window above should give you only the bends you need.

Look from a fresh perspective. How does your customer see it? Walk through the steps only your customer cares about. How does your customer feel?

Don't get bogged down with how you're going to do it and try to ignore what you currently do.

With a clean sheet or wall re-map you most wanted process. At each step write what information needs to be collected to hand on to the next process. Often I've found if the company gathers more information at the start of the process, it removes a heap of questions or customer interactions further along the process.

With one of my clients, a telecoms company, we identified a bottleneck because each new telecom installation had a site survey by one of the installation team, adding time and cost into the process. During the sales process every site is visited by a salesperson. By implementing a smarter sales sheet and with some training the site survey can be conducted by the sales person, saving the extra visit (which would invariably take half a day with travel) and took at least three days out of the process for the customer.

Add Technology

This is probably my favourite bit of the process. Those that know me will have a wry smile because I'm quite techy and I love innovation. But this is where the magic happens. Technology and automation will propel your business forward like you wouldn't believe. So much of what you do can be automated and the process 'systematically driven' rather than waiting for human intervention.

It used to be the norm for a company to write process manuals or Standard Operations Procedures (SOP's) and try to get each member of staff to follow them. As soon as something changed, the manuals or SOP's would need to be amended and new copies re-issued. Now, if you create smart systems, you can push people along the process as the technology tells them what to do next.

Slick modern companies invest in IT. I worked for the Automobile Association during the nineties when they went from having over 15 'radio rooms' (call centre and deployment offices) down to just three serving the whole country. Now most of their operation is completely systemised, with almost zero human intervention apart from the initial call; the patrols are deployed by complex algorithms.

Look at how Uber have shaken up the taxi industry. There's also new banks emerging like Monzo; in just three years they've grown from zero to over two million customers by making banking really simple. They've reduced the cost to serve a customer from £65 down to £30 by using slick technology. But it's their approach and mindset that's really important; they're constantly challenging how they can give a better customer experience and reduce complexity.

These 'disruptors' are investing serious monies to re-invent their industries. Don't get me wrong, I'm not suggesting you should invest anything like that kind of money. But I want you to use the same thinking and approach, and embrace technology. How can you provide a better customer experience and reduce complexity using technology?

It doesn't have to be that expensive, and if anyone suggests building you a bespoke system from scratch, tread very carefully. There are so many free or low cost platforms available which are off-the-shelf, easy to use and easy to integrate with other systems.

You may already have these systems in your business, but when were they last reviewed? These systems should enable a business and not disable it. So many times I've found businesses putting up with systems that aren't fit for purpose any more (or never were).

I want you to imagine a powered conveyer belt. At the start your customer makes an enquiry and from here on, this conveyor belt, with the customer sitting on it, flows through your business. When it gets to each process intersection it slows waiting for the process to happen, and continues only when that process has been completed. No-one has to remember to do anything, the system does most of the easy thinking and 'heavy lifting'. If you go back to the Critical Value Window, we identified those processes which added value to the customer. These are important to your customer and therefore it's how you add value. The focus for your business should be about delivering your value, therefore everything else should either be stopped or done with automation where possible. This is the modern day equivalent of the industrial revolution; machines and systems to automate menial tasks.

Your biggest challenge with business systems will be to get them talking to each other. Fortunately most of these are now cloud based and have 'API' which basically means they can integrate or talk to other applications. It will be very rare if you can find one good system that will support your entire business needs. I know because I've tried for many clients to find them such a thing. What I've found is that one system might do one or two bits really well, their core systems. They try to develop bolt-ons to expand the capability but these seldom work well. I know of operations systems that have developed their own accounting systems, why? There are many really slick and cost-effective accounting platforms out there, why re-invent the wheel?

Without knowing the exact requirements of your business it's difficult for me to advise you what platforms or systems to use. This is also a fast-changing world so rather than list recommended systems here, we'll post it with our tools and try to keep it updated, just go to www.betterneverstops.global/tools).

Train & Implement

One of the biggest mistakes businesses make when implementing new systems and software is to skimp on the training. The business owner (you) will try to save a few pounds by removing or cutting right back on the training. Often the training just consists of a technician loading it onto users PC's and the technician gives the user a ten minute 'this is how you use it' demo. The true power in these systems is normally the little time hacks and shortcuts. Please don't make this mistake. Instead look to find a way to have ongoing training and updates. We all use software differently and often when you sit with someone you'll see them do something and go "Wow, how did you do that?" The one little hack can save hours of work for many people each month, how much is that worth?

Review

Better Never Stops…

When Mercedes win the F1 World Championship do they stop developing their car and team?

Of course they don't. Their ultra-competitive environment dictates that the next race every team will step up to try to beat them. Their business is constant innovation and improvement.

Again I want you to have the same mindset and approach. Just because you've done one round of improvements it shouldn't stop there, it must be a continuous cycle:

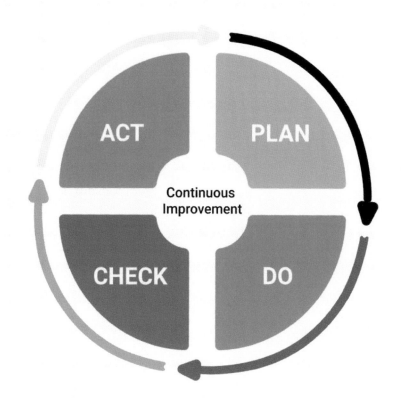

Kanbanize.com

From the new processes you've implemented what were the expected improvements? Once these have settled down and embedded, what has actually happened and therefore what are the new results? How can you improve these? Remember, faster slicker.

- You should constantly strive for continuous improvements and better efficiencies. Bring key people together each month to keep the continuous improvement momentum going. Get the whole team brought into the philosophy by involving them:

- Implement a staff suggestion scheme and ideas board to get them feeding ideas in. Some of these ideas may be off the wall, but sometimes these are the ones that trigger the really great improvements.

- Run process improvement workshops in small teams to get them to re-invent what they do.

- At the start of every day get your team to ask, "What went well yesterday? What didn't go so well? What can we improve today?"

- Work with your customers and suppliers and ask the same question, "How can we take time and complexity out of our shared processes?"

Summary

As I wrap up this chapter I'll share with you a couple of case studies of how I've used this approach with my clients.

The first is a windows, doors and conservatory company.

With the business owner, and a key manager, we set out on a mission to review all the processes within the business. We took over the boardroom for two days and during that time invited at least one person from each department to take us through what they did on a daily basis. Remember, reality is king.

Each person also brought in copies of all the paperwork and sales or operational materials they would use. Once completed, we were shocked with the number of forms and process steps. We found the customer's name was written or typed 12 times.

Now, let's say it takes ten seconds to gather and write a customer's name, and they dealt with over 1,500 customers per year. So: 1500 x 12 x 10 / 60 = 3,000 minutes or 50 working hours spent each year writing a customer's name. The other issue is the potential to write it incorrectly and there's nothing worse than getting someone's name wrong.

By re-mapping the processes, and removing duplication, we saved two days in the process and dramatically reduced the number of forms. In the longer term we managed to reduce headcount by two and provide a better service to customers.

The second case study is a remanufacturing company.

The company employed 21 people and remanufactured around 18,000 units a year. We knew their business needed improving as the number of non-productive staff, versus the productive staff, was far too high which of course had a significant impact on their profitability.

With the business owner and his team, we mapped all their current processes and gathered up all the current paperwork. They have a computerised sales and stock management system but, beyond that, no operational management system. Without manually counting or gathering information they had no instant data which could tell them the operational performance of the business; never knew at any one time how many jobs they had in process, their productivity levels, parts used or stock levels etc. They used an antiquated web based ordering control system to generate job cards and at least five different spreadsheets and numerous paper forms, which were typed back into spreadsheets.

They also have around 2% of units (360 units) returned each year under their no quibble warranty, these were replaced without testing or question in a straight-forward exchange. But, if a labour claim was submitted, these were individually tested and a salesperson would spend two days a month replying to the customers to confirm whether it was valid or invalid, once an internal test procedure was conducted.

We re-mapped the processes and, using Google Sheets and AppSheet, we created an operational management system we called Team Universal. This centralised all the data, removing all of the other spreadsheets and duplication. Using technology, the sales and stock management system 'talks' to Team Universal, which in turn also 'talks' to the courier management system. Most of the required data is only entered once and carried through the process. We also reviewed the warranty process. An online form is now submitted by customers and the majority of the process is automated or completed by a warehouse operative. All in all we saved at least five days of administration per month, reduced the head count by three people and increased productivity by 25%. The investment in technology was around £10,000.

As you can see from these two examples, a great deal can be gained from this approach.

How much could you save in time, cost, complexity? And how much could you gain in a better customer experience?

Just because you've always done it this way don't get constrained by your past and don't allow your business to become fat, lazy and clumsy.

I want you to accept that what you've got here is great and works but, to move forward, the business needs to evolve. Look at your business with a fresh pair of eyes and tap into the entrepreneurial mindset you have.

Adrian Peck

But, this is going to take courage and a time investment to drive the improvements to keep your business ahead of your competitors. If you stand still for long enough you will become a dinosaur and get left behind at a great rate of speed.

SEPARATE

Everyone Can Beat You On Price...Guaranteed.

Yep, you heard it here first.

Every week I hear one or all of these statements from businesses just like yours:

"Our customers are only interested in price."

"We find out how much our competitors are charging, and we beat them on price."

"We've got a good relationship with our customers and they'll tell us what price we've got to beat."

"Our market is different, it's so competitive, customers are driving down our prices and we're just losing margin."

Let's get a few of these myths out of the way:

- Just about every business is in a competitive market.

- Our customers have more choice now than they ever have had before.

- Someone will always sell it cheaper.

But every bit of research on customer behaviour and their purchasing decisions that I've read <u>never</u> puts lowest price as the first buying factor.

Why do so many salespeople and businesses believe price is the most important factor?

Customers will buy on price if you don't show or give them any other reason why your product is different to that of your competitors. Customers are highly trained in looking for "why should I buy from you?" If everyone offers the same product, on the same terms, with the same service or delivery, price becomes the only point of difference.

In most industries, and with most products, just about every product will, over time, become commoditised. If the demand is big enough, someone always finds a way of making it cheaper.

"This is made in China for under half the price that we can make it."

These products hit the UK, the industry goes from worried to full-blown panic, price becomes the only determining factor and it's a race to the bottom. And it's not going to end well for sellers. You've only got to look at the current situation in our high streets to see this for real.

But a few retailers are bucking the trend. One example is Lush. Yes, a store selling very smelly soap. Think of all the places you can buy soap and cosmetics. But Lush doesn't compete on price.

They've grown to know their customer really well, their stores are different and offer a distinctive buying experience, and it works.

You've got brands like Apple. Again, they know their customers very well and their products are rarely marketed on price. Their pricing strategy isn't to be the lowest in the market, but they are a mass consumer brand. People will pay for a perceived higher quality product or service.

You may be thinking, "Yeah, this is all well and good for these big brands, but Adrian we're just this small business, turning over £2m and we can't operate on the same level."

And you're right, you can't operate on the same level. But you can use the same tactics, which will get you a much better market position and, most importantly, improve your margins.

Let's just reflect back for a moment. My purpose in this book is to enable you to Fall Back In Love With Your Business. One of the reasons behind your failing love is "the harder I work, the less I earn." If we can increase the margins in your products you'll earn more money, agreed?

But to do so you have got to stop competing solely on price.

In this chapter I'm going to show you how to separate away from your competitors to create your own market and products. And we're going to cover four steps:

1. Review your current products

2. Identify your target market

3. Research & Development

4. Create your own market

What we need to do is to create a special niche for your business. That niche will be a combination of the products you sell and the people to whom you sell them. I'm not saying for a moment this is a five minute process and in two weeks you're going to be this different company. It's not that simple and, like anything that's ever worthwhile, it will take some hard work and time.

But I can pretty much guarantee that your business is currently leaving money on the table every day with your customers. If you don't offer your customers something different in the market, then without realising it you're going head-to-head with your competitors and lower prices will be the winner.

Product With Service Company

A great friend and cycling buddy of mine and I were having coffee halfway round one of our Saturday morning rides. Paul is the Managing Director of the four largest fuel card brands in the UK. I said to him, "In your market where the price of fuel is critical to your customers, you must be in a constant price war with your competitors?"

His answer surprised me...

"Far from it Adrian, we have the largest number of fuel sites in the UK. It was a strategy of mine way back to provide our customers with the biggest choice of re-fuelling sites. It means our customer has control over their drivers and therefore more control over their fuel spend. We know, for our target market, this is really important, and it keeps us ahead of our competitors."

This is a great example of how you separate from your competitors and create your own market, even with a commoditised product.

Product Only Company

If your company is only supplying products, and if they haven't already, in due course your prices will come under fire. The only exception is that you have some magical unique product only you can make and sell. This is rare and given your market position unlikely to be true for someone reading this book. In the real world, once demand for a new product gets traction, more competitors follow, the market gets saturated, there'll be over supply and prices will come down.

To combat it you must find ways to stay ahead by constantly innovating, spending enormous time and money on R&D.

The easiest and most effective way is to find ways of adding value through services. If you combine products with service your product becomes unique, it will position you away from your competitors and remove the volatility of your business.

Let's look at how we can do this for you…

Review your current products

Before you can improve your products, we first must identify how they are currently performing. For some this might be straightforward and, for others, it's going to be a challenge. Nevertheless, it's an important step and must be done, and for each of your key product offerings we need to know:

1. Past and current sales volumes.

2. Your costs and sales margins.

3. The different customer types you sell to.

4. Potential market opportunity and condition of the market.

5. What are your unique selling points?

6. What are your competitor's unique selling points?

7. Like and hassle scoring.

Product And Market Analysis Tool

Not surprisingly you'll find a special tool on our website, www.betterneverstops.global/tools to help you do this.

I'll walk you through each of the steps above.

1. **Past and current sales volumes**

   What we're trying to ascertain here is past and current volume of sales so that we can identify if the product is still growing, if it's peaked and flat, or in decline. If your volumes are going down but you believe the market is still growing why aren't your volumes?

2. **Your Costs and sales margins**

   How much does it cost you to produce and deliver each product or service and, what is your margin? Just to be clear, as I've found many to get this wrong, there's a big difference between mark-up and margin. If you mark-up a product by

30% it doesn't mean you make 30% profit, in fact you'll only make 23%:

Mark-up

Cost = £50 -> mark-up 30% = £15

Total = £65 -> Profit = £15

£15 divided by £65 (x100) = 23% Gross profit

Margin

Cost = £50 -> 30% Margin = £35 (Multiply cost by 1.7)

Total = £85 -> Profit = £35

£35 divided by £85 (x100) = 30% Gross Profit

3. **The different customer types you serve**

Who are the different customer types you sell to? Are these customer types increasing, staying the same, or reducing? Will there be more, the same or fewer customers to sell to?

4. **Potential market opportunity and condition of the market**

Are there opportunities for you to expand either the types of products or the types of customers? In other words, can you sell more products to your existing customers or can you sell your existing products to different customer types? What are the market conditions for your customers, is the market in a growth stage, stagnant or decline? What's likely to happen in the future? What pressures are your customers under? What's happening in their world? What's going to drive change? Will it bring about positive or negative change? Is there pending or future legislation which will affect the market or affect your customers or your competitors?

5. **What are your unique selling points**

   What makes your product unique in the market? Why would a customer buy from you rather than your competitors? How long can you maintain this?

6. **What are your competitors' unique selling points?**

   What makes your competitor's product unique in the market? Why would a customer buy from them rather than you? If you don't know, go and find out by doing some research. Act as a potential customer and see how you're treated. What information or techniques do they use? How do they present their products? We often do this for our clients.

7. **Like & hassle scoring**

   Do you like providing this product or serving these customers? Does it fit with the company's personality? Is this product or type of customer easy or difficult to serve? Are there some customers who take up an unproportionate amount of time on administration or support?

Using the form you will now be able to score against each of the seven key areas; one is low and five is high. Add the scores and write the total at the end. Normally a couple of products will stand out and these will start to shape your thinking of what to work on. Low scores across all of the rows should serve a warning to the viability of your current markets and products.

Identify your target market

This is probably the one single step that is often ignored by businesses or, at best, given far too little consideration when developing products or marketing. Here's the hard truth and the one thing you MUST get right:

Getting your target market right is the single most important aspect of business success.

You can have the most amazing product but if it's marketed to the wrong people it will never be that successful.

What I'm about to explain to you may chill you to your core. But in order for your business to separate away from your competitors you need to take a piece of the market and own it. Unless your market is very small, and that would be a whole other conversation we'd need to have, you cannot successfully serve your entire market. Doing so just dilutes your products and they will be weak generic 'also rans', and I'm sure this isn't what you want for your business.

Stop trying to sell to everyone. You cannot be all things to all people, you simply haven't got the budget, the time and the resources for it.

The analogy I often use when talking about target markets is fishing. Imagine one of the beautiful large lakes in the Lake District, or an equally beautiful Scottish loch. In this lake or loch are thousands of fish of just about every freshwater variety you can name. Every day you get up early to sit around this lake or loch with hundreds of fishermen who are just like you, you're all competing to catch the most amount of fish. Daily you're all there and you keep catching fish, all using pretty much the same equipment, the same baits and the same methods. And of course, you all catch the same random types and size of fish. Over time you grow smarter and work out that not all fish are equal, catching certain types of fish are much more valuable and rewarding to you.

So you think, "why don't I catch more of those?" But, and here's the scary bit:

1. **You'll reduce the volume of fish you catch.**

2. **You'll need to invest in working out how to catch your right fish.**

And of course you're addicted to catching volume and breaking from this would be very courageous. You get thinking about how rewarding it would be to get up every day, sit around the beautiful lake or loch and only catch the fish you really want. You don't need to waste time catching other fish that sap your time and energy, only for you to eventually throw them back. Over time, and while your competitors keep fishing for everything, you specialise in salmon fishing and become the market leader. A bit later you work out that trout are also caught a similar way and you like catching them. Now you've got two target fish.

We need to get to the heart of your preferred target market.

This is how you've got to think about your business. Who are your Salmon and Trout? What types of customers do you like to deal with and would dearly love more of? Which types of customers would you like to throw back?

Let's just step back a second to make sure we understand what we mean by target market.

A target market is a clearly identified group of people or companies within the total market who:

1. Share similar characteristics or traits such as geography, buying power, demographics, and incomes;

2. Need and want your products;

3. Can afford to pay for your products;

4. Can be reached by marketing activities;

5. Are large enough in volume to warrant investing time, energy and resources to gain a return on investment.

Don't worry, as you've seen with our fishing analogy you can have more than one, in fact you can have several. If you think about a department store and brand like John Lewis, you could argue that their target market is everyone, for indeed anyone can walk into one of their stores or shop on-line and buy their products. But they don't want one customer to buy one product. They want customers to buy lots of products and keep coming back for more. Their target market is aimed at mid to high earning customers but both male and female, and different age groups. In comparison their target market is very different from Primark. John Lewis doesn't stop the 'non target customers' shopping with them, they just choose not to market to them.

I like Ted Baker clothes, but I'm not their target market, their brand is aimed at an audience at least 15 years younger than me. Each season, when they design their clothes, I'm certainly not on their avatar board or in the mind of Ted's designers. They have a very clear understanding of their target market and they stay very close to them to keep their products in tune, and hence their great success. Of course that doesn't stop me buying their clothes but I'm not their target market, they don't spend money marketing to me.

How Does This Work For You?

We need to discover who your perfect target market is and we're going to use two tools, the Customer Identifier and the Your Perfect Customer Matrix.

The first step is to identify the types of customers you serve using the Customer Identifier. On our website you'll find two versions, one for Retail if you sell to consumers (B2C), and one for Business if you sell to companies (B2B).

B2B

If you sell B2B, this is probably going to be slightly easier for you as you'll tend to have a list of all your customers' names. Using the Customer Identifier B2B sheet, copy a list of your top 50 customers in column 'Customer Names'. Your top 50 should be by spend, i.e. the top 50 customers who spent the most money. Using the column headings (Sector, Location, Size etc) work along the columns, which will help you identify the common characteristics and traits. From here you should be able to put your customers into some sort of group or groups.

B2C

If you sell B2C, this is a bit tougher. If you've got a list of customers, again copy and paste your list here and work across the column headers. If you haven't got a list of customers, work with your team to create a list of customer types and group them.

On the next sheet, Your Perfect Customer Matrix, you can rate your different groups. Using the header columns score each group 1 (lowest) to 5 (highest) for the following for each:

- They want your product.

- They can afford your product.

- They will pay a premium for your product.

- You can reach them quickly, easily and cost-effectively.

- There's enough of them to make your business successful.

- Your business already has credibility with them or you can quickly gain credibility.

- Their location allows them to be serviced conveniently and cost-effectively.

- Their market condition, decline or growth; score 1 = rapid decline, 2 = decline, 3 = steady, 4 = growing, 5 = high growth.

The higher the score the more perfect that group is for you, and ideally you've got groups scoring 25 and above.

Research & Development

Using the Separate Workbook, we need to bring the work together to discover how we're going to develop your product or products to:

1. Add value to make them more valuable to your customers;

2. Put clear water between you and your competitors.

Remember the objective here is to Separate; to create your own market of customers.

The one thing we haven't done so far is to talk to your current customers. This is easily overlooked but from experience I can tell you it will provide amazing insights to help you develop your products and services.

1. Put together a questionnaire and send out to your customers and ask some questions like:

    a. Why do you buy from us?

    b. What could we do better?

    c. If you didn't buy from us, who would you go to and why?

    d. What other products (services) would you like us to provide?

    e. What's your biggest challenge at the moment?

2. Talk to your customers and ask the same questions.

3. Collate all the answers (you'll be amazed at the results).

4. Discuss with your team the feedback and use this through the next steps to help develop your products and services.

To further help you, I'll give you three effective development strategies I use with my clients. How could you adapt these for your products and services?

1. Good, Better, Best Options

    The idea here is that you create three versions of your products: a Good but cheaper, Better and slightly higher priced and a Best, which is the premium brand.

    Many of the supermarkets do this with various ranges; ASDA have a Smart price (Good), their ASDA brand (Better) and Extra Special (Best).

    Long haul airlines do it with flights; Economy (Good), Business Class (Better), First Class (Best).

    If you think about ASDA, and let's say it was a cooking sauce, each of the three different products would flavour your sweet and sour chicken.

    Each one of the seat options would get you to New York.

    The difference is the perceived quality and value. How could you use this strategy with your products? How can you add more perceived value to differentiate your products or services for different target markets without incurring additional costs? Do some of your customers want a low cost option? Do others want or expect a high quality option?

2. Packaging or Bundling Products

    Can you package or bundle your products to provide more added value and effectively generate more revenue from each sale?

    Let me give you two well known examples.

    First is packaging: The Happy Meal. Put the food into a themed box, bundle a few products together, add a toy and 'bingo', it's every child's favourite. The products bought separately would be more money, but they cleverly put the range together to guarantee a higher transaction value every time.

The second example is a car wash, they bundle a range of services together and provide a menu of choices, each increasing in price.

How can you package or bundle products together to form single offerings? The object is to add more value and increase transactional profit. Yes, you would get more money if you sold each product separately but realistically, how many times do you sell the whole package? Imagine selling a bundle of products on every sale. Above are simple examples, and that's the thing, they don't need to be overly complicated. Keep it simple.

3. Continuity Programme and Subscriptions

Can you generate additional revenue streams from a continuity programme or by creating a subscription service? Not only do these generate immediate revenue, they'll also increase the value of your business. Investors love to see recurring revenue streams in businesses as a sure way to future-proof sales and provide longevity. These programmes could be to provide products or services or both. Is there an element to your products which needs regular replacement that you could turn into a regularly guaranteed purchase?

For example, you sell water softeners, the regular consumable would be the salt, and every two years the equipment needs a service. When you sell the product you roll up the salt and service into a monthly charge, the customer now has a hassle free service, they get salt delivered to their door and their equipment stays in tip top condition. You've increased your revenue and locked in a potential customer for life.

Create your own market

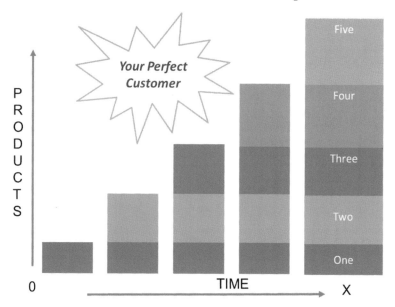

The Customer Stairway

One of the major things about customers and products I've observed when working with clients is how products naturally build over time. When we unpick some of their top clients we see how the relationship developed. Invariably what happened is one day they solved one problem to help a customer (product one). As the relationship grew, they solved problem two (product two) and the customer bought it, and then three etc. Therefore, when you stand back, you realise sales grow as relationships grow. The stronger the relationships, the stronger the sales and number of products (or services) you sell to your customers. But it all started on day one, when you solved one problem. But what we try to do when we sell is present all our products in one hit, and we expect our potential customer to identify the one they want to buy today. This just blinds our customers like rabbits in headlights.

As we develop your products and services, we need to keep the Customer Stairwell in mind to find the products and services that solve a small problem but build a big relationship.

Bringing It All Together

The art of separating away from your competitors is about creating your own market. A market that you know and love, and in time will love you. You understand the customers so well and you have a sales strategy that intelligently builds a series of products that you know your customers need.

Above we have:

- Reviewed your current products.

- Identified key target markets.

- Collated feedback from your existing customers.

- Looked at product development strategies.

We need to bring all the work together to define:

1. Who is going to be your primary target market?

   Using the steps above, your primary target market should have become evident. It is possible you have joint top or close second target markets. You can have more than one as long as you don't try to sell to them at the same time, i.e. you can't have two lines on one fishing rod. Your approach and message will match one target market, otherwise you'll confuse and lose.

2. What products and services are you going to sell to them?

   Based on your customer feedback and development strategies how can you innovate and evolve your products and services? How can you package or bundle them better? Can you develop and test different price tactics?

3. When are you going to sell them?

   For each target market you need to map the Customer Stairwell showing a clear route of how you can sell additional products over a period of time. What product will solve a problem for everyone in this target market? It needs to be as easy as possible for your customer to take this first step.

Summary

The best way I can wrap this chapter up is to give you a working example of how I've implemented the steps above with a client. I've already mentioned this client, they specialise in supplying underfloor heating products. I can't give too much away in terms of their strategy but I'll take you through how they applied the steps above.

1. Review Your Current Products

Sales Numbers – Fortunately they have a sales quoting and order management system, so analysing their data was quite straightforward. What became apparent was that they had very high lead volume, but the quality wasn't great.

Customers – these were roughly split 50/50 between consumers and the trade market. Sales were split 60/40 direct/telephone based, and online. The online market was getting saturated and of course very price driven. The underfloor heating market is a growing market and with the push towards greener homes it will continue to rise.

Unique Selling Points – there was very little to differentiate between suppliers in the market and whilst the competitor research showed my client in a positive light, overall there was plenty of room for improvement.

Like & Hassle – when the sales team discussed the quality of current sales, one of the big issues that came to light was the time consumed with retail customers. Their sales value was often much lower than trade and they required lots of telephone support.

2. Target Market

Apart from spending quite a considerable sum on Google Adwords, they weren't really doing any out-bound marketing. Therefore they didn't have any control of their target markets; they would take any online orders and try to win as much telephone business as possible. By analysing their data they soon worked out who were the better quality customers, and they knew they just needed to get more of them. By proactively marketing, the proportion of unwanted leads would drop, giving them more time to focus on the good ones and sales would increase.

3. Product Development

    Like everywhere else, underfloor heating is very competitive. There's an increasing supply of products from China and many sellers are killing the market with unsustainable prices. They knew they needed to add value by providing services around the products. After researching the customers, they saw that there's a strong enough market for a 'done for you' service where they could add value and not compete on price. Within each of the product ranges they identified an opportunity to offer Good, Better & Best packages to suit different budgets.

4. Create Your Own Market

    Putting all this together they set about increasing the database of potential customers for the new target markets, and set up campaigns to engage with them. For the Customer Stairway they introduced some products to help build a relationship, some free guides and sample packs. Within the sales processes they also created ways to upsell and cross sell as the relationship builds.

Hopefully, I've managed to give you a flavour of what they did. I'm sorry I can't give you the deep detail but I'm sure you can appreciate there's some commercially sensitive information I can't share. Oh, you might also want to know what the effect was? In early 2016, the goal was to double the business in five years. By March 2019, the business has more than doubled in revenue and net profit has gone from a single percentage to over seventeen percent. The growth has mostly been fuelled by having a better quality customer and giving them a great added value service. They will do deals with customers, but they don't compete on price and they will walk away from the wrong sort of business.

SCALE

A good marketing and sales strategy is the secret sauce of every successful business.

As this chapter is all about growing your business you may wonder why I didn't put this chapter first. Indeed it would make sense to grow the business and then worry about getting the rest right. Some readers might even jump straight to this chapter.

But this is where many, many businesses go wrong. Without realising it they try to grow their business out of trouble and simply end up with even bigger headaches.

A business with an outdated structure and approach doesn't change if you add more customers. All you do is put more customers through a bad system and you get a poor return on the money and time you've invested in marketing and sales.

The same can be said for products and customers. I've met many businesses that don't like their customers and are struggling along with products that don't match the owner's ambition.

If you've successfully completed all the steps above, you'll now have a significantly better business. I want you to feel confident that your business is now in the best condition to move forward. I want you to get the greatest possible return on the money and time you're now going to invest in this chapter.

A very common business mistake I see is to only focus on developing or improving marketing and sales when you go quiet. Typically, everyone gets distracted and consumed by what they need to obtain today. Without a consistent and constant marketing plan and sales programme, your sales will cycle from feast to famine. One month you're too busy, so you 'turn the flow down', and the next month sales increase and you 'turn the tap back to full flow'. This puts unnecessary strain on just about every aspect of the business as it jumps from flat out to half power, back to full power etc. You wouldn't drive your car like this. This might sound extreme, but I've come across lots of companies who run like this.

Always selling: the habit of successful companies

Ideally the business should beat to a consistent rhythm. A consistent flow of quality leads, professionally followed-up through tried and tested sales conversion techniques, and every opportunity taken to maximise customer value.

Now, this last one 'maximise customer value' is probably the most powerful and, sadly, the least used strategy in most businesses I meet. Without them, it's like trying to fill a bath with the plug out and with holes drilled in the sides.

You keep pouring water in (sales leads), a certain amount stays (sales conversion) and then it just leaks away again. Without the tap constantly pouring costly leads in, the bath would be empty.

Imagine the bath with the plug back in and only a small hole (or two) half way up the bath. You've sealed all the other holes with customer maximisation strategies. Most of the water stays in and, for you to continue growing, you only need a trickle of leads keeping the bath topped up.

A good marketing and sales strategy is the secret sauce of every successful business. Many falsely believe you need a top-quality, industry-leading product to be successful. But a good product badly marketed will never fly and will soon die. A mediocre product, marketed well, will sell and survive for years.

Is McDonald's a top-class restaurant? Many would argue the food is terrible. But they're probably one of the leading global companies when it comes to marketing and sales.

In this chapter we are going to cover the three principles of successful marketing for any small business:

1. Lead Generation

2. Sales Conversion

3. Customer Maximisation

We've already briefly covered these within the Chapter 4 section CASH, and here I'm going to dive deeper into each of these.

As I explained in CASH, these principles are multipliers: if you improve all three, the impact multiplies through each. Just to remind us, here's the example from above again:

Current			Increase each element by 10%	
Leads		100		110
Sales Conversion	@ 50%	50	@ 55%	60
Order Value	@ £1,000	£50,000	@ £1,100	£66,550
Repeat Orders	@ 10	£500,000	@ 11	£732.050
Total		£550,000		£798,600

Increase = £248,600. The increase isn't 10%, it's a 45% increase.

Yes this example is simplistic and you may feel it's unrealistic but I can assure you it works. I've used and implemented these principles in many businesses and, when brought together, the results each time have been outstanding.

Always selling: the habit of successful companies

In every successful business you'll find a core culture and habit of 'always selling'. Looking at them from a distance, it would be easy to mistakenly believe their success comes effortlessly to them. They have risen to success in no time and customers are somehow cleverly brainwashed into submission, using this strange 'dark art' called marketing. When you study and speak to the business owners this is far from the truth. They achieve it because they have a well-thought-through, constantly tested and executed marketing and sales programme. But here's the thing:

- Constantly tested means they tried things, measured it and changed it until it worked how they wanted it to.

- They made mistakes (see point above).

- They still have the same approach, just on a different scale.

- They all have a sales team. Successful businesses never stop selling and neither should you.

Measure Measure Measure

Number of Leads

Ave. Order Value　　　　Conversion Rate

Sales revenue is driven by three dependent factors: the number of leads, the conversion rate and the average order value. If any one of these reduces, the triangle above will go out of shape. To maintain revenue one or both of the other two must increase.

Of course the only way you'll know this is by measuring. Whilst there are proven formulas to follow, sometimes the results won't be what you expected.

We've already discussed this in CASH and Control but it's worth mentioning again because it's so important.

To become successful at sales and marketing you've got to measure

If you don't already, you must be able to trace every lead and therefore every sale in your business. Get you sales team into the habit of saying, "Can I just ask, how did you find us?" And record the answer against the sale. Test, measure, review.

Your Opinion Doesn't Count

Everyone has an opinion about marketing and branding: does it look good, what about the words we've used? As an entrepreneur you have to be really careful not to let your perfectionism hold back the need to GSD (Get Shit Done). I've seen Managing Directors spend weeks deciding on font styles and colours rather than just get the bloody marketing out there.

Your potential new customer doesn't care about you, the only care and thought in their mind is:

"What's In It For Me?"

That's all they care about. Not your fonts, your colours, the odd word or phrase.

The only question you should have is:

"Did it generate any leads and therefore sales?"

Ultimately that's all you should care about. The only way to know whether it will work or not is to get it out there. Whenever you can, always put at least two horses in the race, i.e. test different copy or graphics. But only change one thing at a time, otherwise you won't know what worked. For example, you do a 1,000-plus leaflet drop in a town. Create two flyers of 500 each, both with the same copy but different graphics, track the difference by using two different phone numbers and measure the calls, and see which was the most effective. The next time, keep your winner and tweak the copy on the test, see who wins. This approach shouldn't stop; it's my Formula One principle:

Test, Measure, Review To Keep Finding Ways To Go Faster

I could write a whole book on Small Business Marketing, it's such a big subject, which is probably why so many entrepreneurs get bamboozled and don't know where to start. While I'm going to get relatively deep into Lead Generation, Sales Conversion and Customer Maximisation I've put a lot more content onto our website.

I'd love to say the approach and methods I'm sharing with you are my invention, but sadly not. The principles of marketing have never changed and many methods that were invented in the 1920s still hold true today. The only thing that changes is the platform you might use. What I'll do here is de-mystify them and give you guidance on how you implement them and in what order.

Customer Maximisation Strategies

You would think the logical place to start is with lead generation, i.e. to grow you must first increase the number of leads. But I want you to think back to my 'Sales Bath' above. The tap represents leads flowing into your sales team. With the plug in and no holes the bath should overflow, but in real life it doesn't because your bath has holes in it. Some businesses have big gaping holes and wonder why, when they turn the taps full on, they still only manage to cover the base.

In reality the most effective way to generate more business is with the people already doing business with you.

- There will be a pile of money you're leaving on the table every day with your customers without realising it.

- It's much easier to sell to existing customers than to new ones.

- When you do sell to a new customer, you'll want to maximise the revenue from day one.

That's why it makes more sense to me to start with Customer Maximisation Strategies.

Let's first define what we mean by Customer Maximisation Strategies.

Legally and morally maximising the revenue and relationship opportunity with every customer you serve.

You want your customers to spend more money on each transaction, more frequently, for longer, and actively refer you to other people.

In this section we're going to cover these five strategies:

1. Moments of Truth

2. Customer Penetration Matrix

3. Up-Sell and Cross-Sell

4. Referrals

5. Fill The Envelope

I've tried to choose the effective Customer Maximisation Strategies which should suit most business types and if you go to www.betterneverstops.global/tools you'll find even more to use.

Moments of Truth

This is one of my favourite marketing strategies. I love being on the receiving end of it and you will soon see why.

The theory exploits a deep rooted human behaviour that we inherently exhibit: the desire to be the first person to share a positive experience with others.

Question:

- What was the last great film you saw at the cinema?

- For the days following, how many people did you tell about it?

- How did you feel when you told them?

The chances are the conversation went something like this:

You: "<Name>, have you seen X film yet?"

Friend: "No I haven't."

You: "You've got to see it, it's brilliant, <reason 1>, <reason 2>, <reason 3> etc…"

How did you feel when you told them? Yep, you wanted to be the first person to tell them about the film and 'sell' the idea that they needed to also see it.

Apply the same behaviour to a different scenario.

Friend: "We thinking about getting a new kitchen."

You: "Have you been to KBB in Ipswich?"

Friend: "No, should I?"

You: "Yes… They did my neighbour's kitchen, it looks really great and he said the service was outstanding. KBB even went back a few weeks later on a courtesy visit just to check everything was OK and to adjust anything if needed."

You are right in thinking that this is a fairly standard, positive endorsement which happens naturally in most good businesses. But what I'm going to share with you is a strategy of how you can encourage this to happen by finding ways of deliberately giving customers a 'WOW' moment that they'll want to share with others.

The 'moments of truth' concept comes from Jan Carlzon, the ex CEO of Scandinavian Airlines, in his book, 'Moments Of Truth'. It explains how he turned the airline into a customer-focused organisation, and from deficit to roaring profits in only a few years.

Along every customer process there are what Jan calls Moments of Truth. These are the interactions or communication points between you and your customer and these can be a positive or a negative experience. If you think about every time you process a customer order, from the sales lead through to a customer follow up in the future, there are numerous interactions along the way. Some of these are planned, some unplanned. The idea is that you work hard to avoid and eliminate negative experiences and make sure each interaction is positive. You deliberately build in WOW moments, little things that will delight your customers and make them want to tell their friends. But here's the important thing, you don't tell your customers about the WOW moments, you keep these up your sleeve as a nice surprise and they go "WOW". Otherwise it's like being told about the 'big shock' in the film, so you're anticipating it and you'll already have a perception about it.

Here's a recent example I experienced in London when my wife and I stayed in a hotel as part of a birthday treat. Having travelled on business for many years you can probably imagine the number of hotels I've stayed in and the variety of moments of truth I've had.

We stayed in the fairly new Andaz hotel in Liverpool Street, it's not a cheap hotel but these days in London not much is. There's a lot of competition in London amongst hotels so the smart ones need to work hard to maximise their customers. These guys blew us away and gave us probably the best experience I've received at a hotel. Here's the highlights:

- They sent an email a few days before, asking if there was anything we needed for our stay:

    - Asked a few details about checking in etc

- Reason for our stay

- What we liked doing whilst in London

■ When we checked in early to drop our bags, our room was ready for no extra charge.

■ We got back late afternoon to find a cake and handwritten birthday card

■ We got back later that evening to find a birthday balloon and a present

These are only little things, but it's how they made us feel and their attention to detail made us go WOW, and hence I'm telling you now. Everything else about the hotel is really nice but there are lots of really nice hotels in London. How much did those little things cost the hotel?

Implementing Moments of Truth

Step One: Set The Scene

Gather a selection of your team together for a mini workshop – you'll need about an hour. If you run out of time schedule a follow up. Explain what you want to achieve, the reason why and how you plan to achieve it, using the steps below.

Step Two: Remove The Negatives

Using the new processes from Chapter Five – Efficiency, review each step from a customer perspective, put your minds and feet into the heads and shoes of your customer. If you need to, get some people to act as customers and walk through the processes:

1. Is there anything you can do to improve the customer experience, i.e. making it easier to contact you?

2. Are there any points along the way that already cause friction with a customer? It might be charges they always grumble about or the way they transact with you. How can you eliminate these? Or if you can't, pre-warn the customer. Most issues with customers are caused by poor communication; 'forewarned is forearmed'.

3. Are there still any unnecessary steps in the process? Perhaps two steps you could combine into one to make it faster, and easier for the customer to deal with you?

Step Three: Time For The WOW

Brainstorm what things you could do to make them go WOW.

A common mistake we make is that we tell customers "It will be ready in 2-3 days' time." What time do you think they hear? Yep, two, so anything longer than two is negative. Here's a simple WOW moment, tell them four days, and deliver in three. Now you're a day early, and they'll tell people "they delivered it to me a day early."

Do this within your process. Deliberately 'under promise and over deliver' but please do NOT tell them "well we say four but we always deliver within two."

These don't need to be big things, some of my clients send a little pack of Haribos out with every order they ship.

Encourage the team to talk about positive experiences they've had and how it made them feel. How can your business do that?

Step Four: Putting It All Together

Review your processes, making the improvements to eliminate the negative and friction, and add in the WOW. Make sure that when you implement this you train your team well about the new changes and the need to WOW.

Step Five: Better Never Stops

Each month schedule an hour with your team just to work on WOW moments. Keep walking through the steps above; review, improve, WOW and implement.

Customer Penetration Matrix

How many of your customers could buy all your products? How many know about all the products you sell?

If you don't know, don't worry, you're not alone, this is fairly typical in most businesses. And of course there's always the assumption "I'm sure our customer must know that we also do…"

Here's a great way to make sure all your customers know about all of your products and, where possible, buy these from you, increasing sales, profit and the depth of your relationship with them.

You'll need to use the Customer Penetration Matrix you'll find on our website (www.betterneverstops.global/tools).

Here a small version below:

Customer Penetration Matrix

Customer Name	A		B		C		D		E		Product to Customer Pentration %
Co Ltd 1	Y	▾	Y	▾	Y	▾	O	▾	O	▾	60%
Co Ltd 2	Y	▾	Y	▾	Y	▾	O	▾	O	▾	60%
Co Ltd 3	Y	▾	Y	▾	Y	▾	O	▾	O	▾	60%
Co Ltd 4	Y	▾	Y	▾	N	▾	O	▾	Y	▾	75%
Co Ltd 5	O	▾	Y	▾	O	▾	O	▾	N	▾	25%
Co Ltd 6	O	▾	Y	▾	O	▾	O	▾	N	▾	25%
Co Ltd 7	O	▾	Y	▾	O	▾	O	▾	N	▾	25%
Co Ltd 8	Y	▾	Y	▾	O	▾	O	▾	Y	▾	60%
Co Ltd 9	Y	▾	Y	▾	Y	▾	O	▾	O	▾	60%
Co Ltd 10	O	▾	Y	▾	N	▾	O	▾	Y	▾	50%
Customer To Product Penetration	60%		100%		50%		0%		43%		

Here's how to make it work:

1. Across the top list your products.

2. In the first column under Customers, copy and paste a list of all your customers. If you've got thousands you'll need to approach this differently by just analysing a good sample, at least 50.

3. Working across a row:

   a. Has the customer purchased the products from you? Under each mark put a Y for Yes.

   b. If they haven't, but there's an opportunity to sell the product to them, mark O for opportunity.

   c. If they haven't purchased, but it's not possible for the customer to purchase, mark N for No. This will be where a product isn't suitable for all customers or you know they do that in-house already.

4. This is now a 'live' document and your mission is to turn every O into a Yes. It's worth working out how much it would be worth to the company if you turned all the Os into sales, and set a goal with the sales team to hit a target within a timeframe.

5. Working with the sales team, how are you going to contact the customers to encourage them to buy these products from you? What offers or incentives could you use with your customers?

6. As you speak to each customer about the Os update the matrix with an L = Failed to sell opportunity or W = Won new opportunity with customer.

7. Each month meet with your sales team to review, improve and implement... Better Never Stops.

I did this exercise with a telecoms company, it was a big piece of work for the sales team with well over 600 customers. But they contacted just about each one to increase their penetration where they could, and it generated a serious amount of revenue for them.

Up-Sell and Cross-Sell

How can you increase the value of each order by up-selling or cross-selling to them?

This is the same thing as above but you encourage it at point of sale.

Up-sell is increasing the volume of the order by adding value but without adding much cost to you. The classic at McDonalds is "do you want to go large?"

Cross-sell is adding additional products at the point of purchase. Again, at McDonalds, "Would you like a drink with your order?" How could you use these in your business?

There's a perception that when your customer has made a purchase that you should back-off because they won't want to spend any more money. In fact, studies have proven that this is the perfect time to cross-sell and up-sell; they're in a buying frame of mind and they've got their payment card in their hand. It time to add more value…

Up-sell & Cross-Sell Ideas

Here's five ideas for you (there's a load more on the website):

1. Luxury Up-sell

    Can you add a luxury or premium product to your offerings? This is the classic roped-off area or speedy boarding. The net cost to you is very small but high perceived value to the customer.

2. Multi-buy Discount

The supermarkets are very good at doing this. The idea is that you increase the order value of the transaction and still maintain a healthy overall profit. It does reduce your overall gross profit percentage. But you've got to look at it as extra revenue you wouldn't have had and use it wisely on products with high margins. For example:

Discount Up-sell Examples	Price	Profit
Product A	£10.00	£5.00
Discount Up-sell Price for 2	£17.50	£7.50
Discount Up-sell Price for 3	£25.00	£10.00

3. Buy One Get One Free

BOGOFs as they're called. You're reducing the gross profit of the product, therefore it's very similar to the above. You need to be careful to choose products with good margins. The main reasons to use this strategy are:

- To increase product loyalty by getting your consumer to use more of it.

- To promote a new product.

- To re-energise an existing product.

- To add value or promote a complementary product, i.e. you sell a tool with a 'BOGOF' on the consumables.

Ideally these should be 'limited time' offers, which generally creates an urgency to buy them now. You can do the same with subscriptions, where you increase the membership time from one year to 18 months or two years, for an extra charge.

4. Bundled Package

This is a kind of hybrid of Up- and Cross-Sell. The idea is that you bundle or package products together which you might not have sold together. Although you may decrease your overall profit by offering the products at a lower price (when sold together), normally you would have only made the sale on one product.

Package Up-sell Example	Price	Cost	Profit
Product A	£100.00	£50.00	£50.00
Product B	£75.00	£40.00	£35.00
Product C	£60.00	£30.00	£30.00
Total Cost If Bought Separately	£235.00	£120.00	£115.00
Package Cost (all together)	£199.00	£120.00	£79.00

5. POS Cross-Sell

This is when the customer comes to the counter to pay where there's either products placed by the till to encourage extra items to be put in the basket or the assistant will ask "would you like X to go with that?"

The opportunities are endless.

Online you can have recommendations at the check-out, i.e. 'previous customers purchased X with this item', or 'add this to your product'.

Referrals

Again, a simple but effective way to increase your business is to ask your customers for referrals. If you've given them exceptional service full of WOW moments, this should happen quite naturally. But that's a passive uncontrollable strategy and a much smarter way is to create opportunities and habits of always asking or encouraging your customers to pass referrals.

There are three types of referral programmes:

1. Non-Incentive – you just ask and there's no reward offered to the customer. After every transaction ask your customer, either verbally or in writing, (voucher, written on the bottom of the invoice or email), "thank you for your order and your business. Is there anyone you know who could benefit from the products we've provided to you today?" If you've given your customer a really great experience, they are normally only too willing to tell others.

2. Incentive Reward Programme – a reward or benefit offered programme.

    You offer customers a reward for referring customers to you. You can offer two-way rewards, so that the friend gets an introductory offer and the original customer also gets a reward.

3. Silent Reward Programme – You use the same tactics as a non-incentive programme and use the power of WOW. The

idea is that you don't tell your customers about any rewards, instead you give them a nice surprise with a gift and make it as personal as possible.

Which one would best suit your business?

A word of warning: be very careful if you offer discounts on your core products as a reward for referrals. This potentially de-values your product and says "hey, we've got lots of profit in our product." The better way is to offer discounts on up-sell products as this exposes your customers into enjoying enhanced products they might not have used before.

My preference is always option three. If you work B2B, why not try to find referrals for them as a thank you? Actively look through you customer list and see if you can do some matchmaking.

Fill The Envelope

Here's a great low cost way to sell more to people who are already buying from you, you see the likes of Amazon using this a lot. You'll notice when you get a delivery from them, that inside will be offers for other products. Some of these go straight in the bin, but if the offers are strong enough many will stick. Of course there's no delivery cost on your promotional pack because it goes out with the item already being delivered.

1. If you send products to your customers how could you 'fill the envelope'?

2. Could you work with a referral partner who shares the same target market and offer to put an offer out with yours and they do likewise for you?

I also think this could work for customers you visit or visit you, why not give every customer a thank you pack, a simple envelope or even a leaflet with offers and information about other services? Again, could you work with a referral partner?

This would be a great way of distributing a monthly newsletter about your business.

Hopefully I've given you lots of ideas for Customer Maximisation Strategies and there's even more on our website, www.betterneverstops.global/tools

If you implement one or many of these, you will be better placed to maximise every customer opportunity. We can now move on to Lead Generation, one of my favourite subjects.

Lead Generation

I'm mindful that I shouldn't give you so much content your brain goes into overload meltdown. Good Lead Generation will save you hours of wasted time and heaps of lost money. On our website (www.betterneverstops.global/tools) I've provided in depth 'how to' guides and here we'll focus on the practical strategies.

Just to be clear, when we talk about Lead Generation, this means direct marketing strategies that will get your prospects to raise their hand and say "Yes, I'm interested."

Many small business owners wrongly think it's all about building a brand. "We need to get our name out there." Sorry, but this is complete crap.

Brand marketing is for companies with deep pockets.

Don't get me wrong, branding, i.e. having a professional look and consistency across your business, is important. Try anything more than this and you'll waste enormous amounts of money and time.

Lead Generation is an investment in your business, not a cost. You are investing money to generate more business, therefore just like any investment it must be measurable, so you know what return on investment you get. If you can't measure it, it's not an investment. Branding and 'getting our name out there' is not measurable and does not provide a direct return on investment.

These Lead Generation Strategies are for businesses who want to spend time and money to get a direct return on investment.

For direct marketing to work you must have a clear:

Market Message Match

You must know who your target market is, how to get their attention and what you need to say to them to take action.

Target Market

We've already gone through this in detail in the previous Chapter Six: Separate. But it's so important I want to just cover it again and look at it from a marketing perspective. We've already done some exercises which should have you laser-focused on identifying your target market. Everything you do to generate leads for your business should be focused on one target market at a time. And remember, you can have more than one, but the golden rule is you only ever talk to one at a time.

To have effective Lead Generation Strategies we need to know:

- How to find your target market

- Or, where do they look when they need your product?

Ideally you need to know both but you must know at least one. If you don't know at least one, your target market is just a wish list.

Message

Once you know who your target market is, it's all about AIDA:

Attention – you get their attention

Interest – you spark interest from them

Desire – your product appeals to them

Action – you get them to take action

By being 'laser focused' your marketing will win because:

1. Your copy and messages will talk directly to them and tell them what they need to know.

2. You can articulate the benefits homed in to them so they'll instantly understand what's in it for them.

3. Your message won't get diluted by trying to talk to everyone.

4. By deliberately talking to the right people you will discover who you should eliminate and stop wasting time on them.

Your primary goal, within your Lead Generation, is for your target market to instantly think "they're talking to me" and "they really understand my…" and they take action.

The opposite is when you try to talk to everyone. The power of your message will get lost in confusion, it will be difficult to work out and you'll end up talking to no-one. If you confuse you lose. How many times has your brain tried to make sense of an advertisement and just gone, "this is too hard, next…"?

Lead Generation Channel

Here's why it's so important to get your target market right; because if you don't the lead generation channels you'll choose will be completely wrong. Remember, to get it right you need to know where your target market looks or how to find them. Below is a list of the possible lead generation channels split into two sections:

Looks: this is where your target market would go if they were looking for your product or to solve the problem you can fix. They know they have a problem.

Find: this is where you can find your target market, where they 'hang out' but at the time they're probably not looking for your product or solution.

The table below is all of the current lead generation channels I can think of, I don't think I've missed any.

Your job is to go down each channel, keeping your target market in mind, and tick the ones that you feel are applicable, i.e. this is where your target market would look or you could

find them here. This can be downloaded from our website
www.betterneverstops.global/Tools

	Target Market		
Lead Generation Channel	One	Two	Three
Look			
Web search			
Web Directory			
Trade Show			
Exhibition			
Joint Ventures			
Search Engine Optimisation			
Find			
Social Media			
Sponsorship			
Email/Text Campaigns			
Postal			
Advertising			
Press Releases			
Networking			
Seminars			
Telephone Campaign			

Adrian Peck

To help you I'll run through each of the channels above, but before I do that let's just discuss websites.

Firstly, there are three different types of website:

1. E-commerce: its sole purpose is for people to buy things from you.

2. Sales Conversion: the most common sort of non-e-commerce site. Most websites are just glorified sales brochures. The chances are people will go there when they respond to other forms of lead generation to check you out, hence it's a sales conversion, because they are already interested.

3. Call To Action or Funnel Pages: these are lead generation pages which are focused on getting the reader to take one action and fall into a sales funnel.

Secondly, just because you have a website, it doesn't mean you'll get traffic or leads from it. The web is a vast beast, your potential customers are not going to just stumble across you. If you want your site to generate leads you will need to invest in Search Engine Optimisation and Pay Per Click marketing to generate traffic. And for your site to generate true leads it will need very precise and repeated call to actions, i.e. instant quote.

Don't get fooled into thinking "I have a website therefore the people will come".

Where People Look:

- Web search Pay Per Click Advertising – like Google Adwords campaigns. This is where you are going to invest in advertising to drive search traffic to your site based on keywords that the prospects will enter in the search bar. **Don't try to do this yourself.** You'll need a specialist to maximise returns or you'll just burn through a load of cash.

- Search Engine Optimisation (SEO) – potential customers will find you organically if you're local and you've optimised your site for Google Local. Otherwise, you must invest in someone optimising your site for you, and have ongoing activity to maintain a healthy presence through blogging or news updates.

- Web Directory – there are many subscription-based directories such as Trust The Trader etc.

- Trade Show – if you deal B2B the chances are there will be local or national tradeshow events for you. Do your research to make sure your target market does attend, and in enough numbers. To do this right normally requires a high investment in time and money.

- Exhibition – I'm thinking here about consumer-type shows, i.e. Ideal Home, Crufts etc, or many local events and county shows. As above, do your research and visit before you invest.

- Joint Ventures – A very underused but super-powerful channel. Think about your target market, what type of supplier would most likely deal with them, and whether before or after you. Who could you partner with to share marketing and sales costs, and refer each other's business?

Where You Can Find Them:

- Social Media

  The main ones currently are Facebook, Linked-In, Instagram, Twitter, YouTube. You need to decide which platform your target market is most likely to use. If you don't know, do your research or find a social media expert. Each platform is different in terms of the style of content and how you 'sell' on it. And all have pay per click advertising. My advice: only choose one or two to promote on and find someone to manage it for you.

- Sponsorship

  I'm not a big fan of sponsorship because it's difficult to quantify leads from it. This goes back to my point earlier, if you can't measure it, it's not an investment so don't do it. Some very closely related sponsorship works, such as when the business trades with a sport, i.e. a supplier who trades with the competitors such as a bike shop supporting a cycle event. More often it's for community or charitable reasons business owners sponsor teams or events. And of course that's fine, but don't put it into your marketing budget and expect a direct return. You're better putting it in with charitable donations.

- Email/Text Campaigns

  Have a healthy list of opted-in contacts who you can regularly communicate with by email and text. There are still some very effective ways to build lists and, once built, it's one of the most powerful channels at a low cost.

- Postal

I'm a big fan of direct mail marketing. It's not cheap these days but, used well, can be very effective. How many pieces of mail have you received in the last five days? How many emails have you received? How much of the mail did you open or at least take notice of versus the number of emails you read? Can you see how potentially powerful it is? See the lead generation strategy below, Chunky Mail.

- Telemarketing

  I'm not a fan of cold calling but I really like using telemarketing to follow up direct marketing campaigns – "The fortune is in the follow up." Again there's more on this below in Chunky Mail.

- Advertising

  This is quite an odd one these days. It very much depends on your target market and what they are reading. If you're not sure ask them. Printed materials are in sharp decline but some local publications are still going strong. I'm not sure about other counties, but in Suffolk there are some good, low cost local publications delivered door to door.

- Press Releases

  As above, it does depend on your target market and the type of PR you can get coverage in.

- Networking

  From experience, networking is either very good or very bad with not much in between. Organisations like BNI still have the best model, but it's not for everyone. Like most things, you have to be prepared to put a lot of effort in. I'm also involved with Fore Business which mixes Golf and Networking. There are lots of other BNI copies and informal networking groups but be very mindful of 'non-committal' nice groups. I've met lots of serial networkers wanting a return with zero effort.

- Seminars

  Like above they can be good, particularly if you or your company can get a speaking part.

Lead Generation Strategies

I'm going to share with you three tried and tested lead generation strategies that I have implemented with many clients and have achieved great results with. These are proven marketing techniques that have worked for decades.

Chunky Mail

The first one is what I call chunky mail. It's an old favourite used since the 1920s using a traditional direct letter but adding something chunky in the envelope. Why would you do that?

Remember back to AIDA: Attention, Interest, Desire & Action. When you send out a direct mail campaign you've got three major hurdles to overcome:

1. Get the letter opened by the right person.

2. Get the reader to read some of the content.

3. Get the reader to do one of your desired actions.

How this works for a Chunky Mail Campaign:

Attention: get them to open the letter. If someone sends you a sample pen, you know it's a pen but you still open the envelope even when you don't need to order any. **Put something in the envelope to get their attention and open the envelope.** Ideally all envelopes should be handwritten in blue ink for a personal feel. Black ink is for business, blue is personal. OK for large volumes handwritten envelopes won't work but always use blue.

Interest: the item in the envelope should be something they weren't expecting from you, i.e. you'd expect a pen company to send you a pen, but not a bar of chocolate. You want to spark the recipient into thinking "Why has someone sent me this?" and therefore want to read the letter. The headline and first paragraph of the letter should make a link between the gift and why you sent it to them, you now have their attention and interest.

Desire: within the copy of the letter you articulate their problems and how you can solve them, and most importantly "what's in it for them", how they're going to feel afterwards (benefit statements). Always focus on emotions because we buy with our emotions.

Action: the final part and objective of the letter is for them to take action. What do you want your reader to do when they read your letter? Your most wanted outcome (MWO). With some campaigns we've run, the MWO was just for the reader to take our call when we followed up by phone.

The fortune is in the follow-up...

Most B2B campaigns we run are always followed up by phone calls. I always see the two hand-in-hand. With a good follow-up campaign the response rate can easily go over 10%.

If you don't do the telephone follow-up, instead use a series of letters or postcards sent out within days of the first mailing that focuses on the call to action.

A few successful campaigns we've run:

- Lottery tickets

- Curly Wurly Bars

- Kit Kats

- Headache tablets (empty boxes and small foil packs)

If you go to our website you'll find guides on writing effective direct mail campaigns.

Email Campaign Free Guides & Scorecards

This strategy has been used many times within email campaigns with the guide or scorecard as the Action or MWO.

Attention: use powerful subject lines to get them to open the email. The only way to build powerful subject lines is by using good email marketing platforms like Mailchimp. They allow you to run split campaigns to test your subject lines and increase your open rates. Remember your opinion doesn't matter.

Interest: the headline and the first sentence must make the reader think "tell me more", you now have their attention and interest.

Desire: within the copy of the email you articulate their problems and how your guide or scorecard can help solve them, again "what's in it for them". Remember, always focus on emotions.

Action: the final part and objective of the email is to get them to click on the link to download the guide or get the scorecard.

Using the email marketing platforms you can create a series of follow up emails tailored to their response to the first or subsequent emails.

Again there are further guides to sending effective email campaigns on our website, www.betterneverstops.global/tools

Facebook Competitions

This isn't going to suit every target market but I'll take you through a campaign we ran for a Bridal Shop. Within the Facebook platform you can run advertising to very specific target markets. You can also run what are now called 'contests' where you create campaigns to your target market to build your own audience. You have follow up campaigns to build relationships with your audience.

Attention: strong images and messages on their timeline, draw their attention and click to your competition page.

Interest: once on the competition page reaffirm the 'prize'.

Desire: within the copy of the page articulate the prize and how they can win, "what's in it for them", how are they going to feel afterwards (benefit statements). Remember emotions are king (or queen in the Bridal Shop case).

Action: the final part and objective of the page is for them to enter, which in our case was by entering their email address, and accepting the T&C's.

The prize was to win a wedding dress up to the value of £1,000. It was a genuine prize which we ran twice in about a six month period. The cost of the dress and the advertising was around £1,000 each time and across the two campaigns we generated at least £20,000 in sales. Even the winners bought more expensive dresses and accessories which meant the campaigns broke even on their sale alone. The brides agreed to tell their story which became a feature and provided lots of content. Every person who entered got a nice surprise, a £50-off voucher to spend in store when they spent at least £200, and who spends less than £200 in a bridal shop?.

Above I've given you, hopefully, a few useful ideas of lead generation strategies and campaigns. Like I've already said I could write a whole book on marketing, so you'll find lots more useful content on our website www.betterneverstops.global/tools

Sales Conversion

The third and final section in this chapter is the second corner of the Sales Revenue Triangle, Sales Conversion Rate.

I see so many businesses and sales people failing to do this step well. Common mistakes are:

- Poor qualification of lead.

- Delay in responding.

- Not responding.

- Poor quality of sales quotes or presentation.

- Leading with "Let me tell you about us, we were established…" Your customer doesn't care about you, they only care about "What's in it for me?"

- Not listening to, or really not caring too much about, what the customer wants.

- None or very little follow up.

I'll share with you three effective Sales Conversion strategies that continue to work for my current and past clients:

1. Have an effective Sales Funnel.

2. Qualify your leads.

3. Ask for the order.

Again there are more on our website: www.betterneverstops.com/tools.

Like all of the strategies in this book, they are all about following a system and measure, review, improve, because Better Never Stops…

Measure

We covered measuring Sales Conversion above but it's worth going over it again here because it will probably put it in better context here.

If you don't measure it you can't manage it.

I've mentioned this many times already, but how can we continue to improve?

You should already be measuring the number, source and type of leads the business is generating. To improve sales conversions you need to measure:

▪ The value of the lead

▪ The duration from enquiry to closed

▪ Number of touches

▪ Won or Lost

▪ Reason for lost

When it comes to analysing your results, the information above will help you identify Sales Conversion by:

- Source, Value & Type.

- How duration and value effects conversion.

- Reason's you're not converting by source, value and type.

These will all play a vital role in fine tuning your sales systems and approach.

What Is Sales Conversion?

Lead Generation is about getting your prospects (potential customers) to hold their hand high in the air to say "I'm interested".

Sales conversion is about turning these prospects into paying customers. This is often referred to as a Sales Funnel.

A Sales Funnel can be one step:

Here we have a retail customer who responds to lead generation, obtains a quote and buys.

A Multi Step Funnel

BUY

You can see that the first step was to download a guide, followed by a scorecard, a phone call, a proposal and then the customer buys.

Typically the higher the price of the product, the more steps there should be in the process.

Sales Conversion always reminds me of the quote about golf:

"Driving for show, putting for dough" – you might be able to hit the ball a long way but it's all about getting the ball in the hole.

Here you can be brilliant at generating fabulous leads but get your sales conversion wrong and you'll turn few into money. In reality this where you get your return on investment. This is the engine room in your sales department.

Have An Effective Sales Funnel

Within the chapter Efficiency we've already looked at your end-to-end business process. We talked about getting your customer as quickly round the track as possible by removing any unnecessary bends to reduce friction (complexity) and increase speed. Here, we're going to focus on your sales processes to build your sales funnel, ensuring your sales system is optimised for converting your leads into paying customers.

There have been many studies conducted in the number of 'touches' you need to make with a prospect in order to make a sale. I've read some pieces that talk about seven to eleven being the optimum. But most companies stop at one, or at the most three. Just take a moment to think about recent times when you have made a significant purchase. How many times did you chase for a quote? How many times did they follow-up? How efficiently were you dealt with?

Of course the importance here is to be better than your competitors, so, how do you compare?

You need a well-thought-through sales funnel so that every lead the business generates is systematically processed. But don't forget your MOTs (Moments of Truth). MOTs aren't just for customer maximisation, these should also be used during your sales processes. Each contact with a customer should be positive and with strategic WOWs dropped in to delight your prospect.

How to Build Your Sales Funnel

Step One: Select Your Target Market

You should have different funnels to suit each target market and each product type. Yes, you'll end up with multiple funnels, some may only have slight tweaks, but one size doesn't fit all.

Step Two: Map Process & Stages

Walk through each stage, writing down what needs to be done, and the type of activity that needs to happen. These can be a meeting, telephone call, visit to store or home visit etc.

Step Three: Remove friction and add MOTs

Make sure each customer's touch point is positive and brainstorm with your team as to how you can add WOWs.

Step Four: Marketing Media

Pre-write templates such as follow-up emails and letters with strong "what's in it for me?" copy. Remember the prospect doesn't care about you. Include sales brochures and schematics outlining your sales steps so that your potential customer knows what's going to happen.

Step Five: Testimonials

Create a library of previous happy customers categorised by customer and product type. This will provide heaps of reassurance and certainty to prospects.

Step Six: Magic of 7

This is a bit weird, but I'll put it out there. There's a great deal written about a strange phenomenon with the number seven. It's very strongly suggested that by using the number seven in your pricing, it can increase your conversion. Of course, the only way you'll know if it works is by testing.

Step Seven: Test, Measure and Improve

You should be used to this by now, Better Never Stops...

Qualify Your Leads

If you've got your 'Market Message Match' right and your lead generation strategies are working in perfect harmony you should be getting better quality leads.

But none of this is a perfect science and you will still get leads that might not be right for the business. Sometimes it may be the prospect just isn't at the right stage yet. Others are just not the right type of customer.

There are many people out there who will happily suck hours of time from your business and never buy anything or buy very little. While your sales team is distracted with these they are most probably missing out on focusing on high quality customers who do want to do business with you.

The secret is to qualify leads better and therefore throw out the poor quality ones.

Think back to our fishing analogy, we want to ensure you catch the right fish.

How Do You Qualify Enquiries Better?

Within your sales funnel think about the questions you could ask that would eliminate the wrong type of prospects at the sales conversion stage. These could be questions like:

- If you were to go ahead when would you be placing an order?

- What is your budget?

- Are you ready to buy and needing a quote or just thinking about it and needing an estimate?

Make sure within your sales process that your sales team asks these questions as early as possible. You'll get resistance from your sales team on this, they'll perceive they'll miss out or the customers won't give them the information. If you've got a flow of good quality leads, and these leads are genuinely interested in buying from you, they will respond and those that don't are most probably your time wasters.

I had this scenario with a building materials company client, they had quite high volumes of enquiries but a very poor conversion rate. When we investigated, we found the non-converting leads were only getting dealt with by email and never spoken to by phone. The trouble was most quotes took time to generate and the process was made worse by email tennis as the lead wouldn't take phone calls (or that was what we were told).

With resistance, we put in place a process to ask questions before creating a quote. Every new customer, or one that had not previously placed an order before, had to be spoken to on the phone before a quote was provided. We agreed on a script of key questions and implemented the process. Within three months:

- The number of quotes reduced by over 27%

- The sales conversion rate increased from 25% to 52%

- The average over value increased from £2,324 to £3,647

The sales team were able to focus their time more on the larger projects and therefore the average over values increased. The greatest results were in the sales team. There's a better rhythm and atmosphere, their work-load has reduced and it's all much more manageable.

Asking For The Order

This probably is as basic as it gets for any strategy here, but few companies do it and, when they do, it's done terribly. They simply don't ask for the order. They tiptoe around it: "If you want to go ahead, give me a call" or "I'll leave it with you" or "Once you've got the other quotes back, give me a call."

Just about every sales team says something along the lines of "Our customers like us because we're not pushy." In reality, sales people are only human and, as such, have a fear of rejection.

But here's the thing, most customers want to be led and just need help to decide. It doesn't have to be pushy and you just need to ask the bloody question:

- "Shall we go ahead?"

- "If you'd like to secure that price, I can take a small deposit by card now."

- "What card would you like to pay with?"

- "Is there any more information you need to make a decision?" "No." "Would you like me to dispatch that today?"

- "Based on what you've told me, you want this order delivered to you by 30th June, for us to achieve this for you we'll need your confirmation by next Monday, are you in a position to confirm now?"

- "We're getting low on stock for that item, I would recommend you place your order today."

See, none of these are hard and certainly not pushy.

Summary

A good marketing and sales strategy is the secret sauce of every successful business.

I wanted to reiterate this point because it is so important. Successful companies have marketing and sales at the heart of their business and they are always selling.

If you implement the strategies above your business can beat to a consistent sales rhythm: a regular flow of quality leads, professionally followed-up through tried and tested sales conversion techniques, and every opportunity taken to maximise customer value.

The one thing we haven't spoken about during this chapter has been how much you need to invest in marketing and sales. Ignoring Lead Generation for a moment, how much investment will the Customer Maximisation and Sales Conversion strategies above need? Most of them are zero or low. Yes, you'll need to invest some time but not much else.

Remember back to the sales bath. At the moment you will be investing time, resources and money trying to fill your bath with the holes in it. If you implement the Customer Maximisation and Sales Conversion Strategies well, you won't need to have the 'lead taps' on full flow. Therefore, you can reduce the number of leads and your Lead Generation investment will reduce. That said, as a rule of thumb for a high growth business, you should be investing between eight and twelve percent of your revenue back into marketing.

And what's the cost if you don't invest? There's a very high chance your competitors will invest and your business will get left behind. So implementing the strategies above must surely be a 'no-brainer'.

As I've stated many times in this book, business is a team sport, so get your sales team involved and therefore brought into implementing these strategies. You will have heaps less resistance if you can get them brought into the development of sales early on.

And make sure you get the full 'Multiplier Effect' by implementing all three Scale principles. As I explained, the impact of positive improvements multiplies so a small lift in one amplifies the other two.

One last thing. When it comes to creating the marketing aspects, unless you employ an expert marketer inhouse, use a trusted outsourced partner. Don't get fooled by thinking a good salesperson can do marketing as well.

1. Very rarely can they do both very well and one will become a distraction to the other. Get your sales guys involved in the strategy because they should know and understand their customers, but leave the marketing creation to the experts. Leads should be generated by your marketing and the sales team should be focused on converting leads.

2. Everyone has an opinion about marketing and branding, and trying to create it by committee will not work. The only opinion that counts is your potential customer's. Your potential new customer doesn't care about you, their only care and thought in their mind is: "What's In It For Me?" That's all they care about. Not your fonts, your colours, the odd word or phrase.

3. Getting your marketing to generate quality leads is the only outcome you need. "Did it generate any leads and therefore sales?" Ultimately that's all you should care about. The only way to know whether it will work or not is to get it out there and remember: **Test, Measure and Improve.**

MAKING IT HAPPEN

Wow, we've been on quite a journey together and hopefully I've earnt enough respect from you that you won't mind me being quite blunt and direct with you.

The reason we've got all the way through this book together is because you're not happy with the current state of your business and in turn how it's affecting your life. You've recognised the symptoms I described in the introduction that are also causing you to fall out of love with your business.

I've shown you a proven way to improve your journey and make the necessary changes to fall back in love with your business.

As I see it, you're now at a road junction with three possible route choices:

Route One – Turn around and go down exactly the same road again and in essence take nothing from the seven SECCESS® steps above and do absolutely naught.

And surprisingly, you won't be alone, many won't do anything different. You'll carry on seeking the magic wand, the magic pill or the promise of the entrepreneur's secret that will cure your business. Or you'll carry on with your head in the sand hoping something will just happen.

You're an entrepreneur, you're tough, resilient and driven to succeed. You've only got this far and built your business to what it is by making shit happen. Now is no different, things are only going to change if you make it happen. Otherwise shit will happen to you.

Please don't be the person who blames everyone for your situation. That's not you, you're made of stronger stuff and you know deep inside life is a series of choices and you're in control. The worst decision you can make is to ignore your choices and do nothing.

Take control…

Route Two – Take action by implementing the steps above. I really hope you do because I know the steps above will change your business and change your life. Very quickly your business will be transformed; it will be easier to manage, you'll feel rejuvenated and quickly start to fall back in love again with your business.

Don't forget to use the all the tools and extra content available on our website: www.betterneverstops.global/tools. I'm constantly uploading new exciting stuff to help in any which way I can so make sure you subscribe to the updates and I'll email you when we add new content. I'll also email every week with hints and tips to help keep you motivated and on track.

Please reach out if you need help or clarification, or just some moral support. On our website you'll find lots of ways to get in touch.

Route Three – Get some help. This will take some courage because we have this strange belief system that tells us that by asking for help we've failed, or we shouldn't need to. The reality is, asking and using help will be the most liberating and motivating action you can take. Knowing you need help and using it wisely is a sign of strength, not weakness. For hundreds of years, leaders and entrepreneurs have sought counsel from people they trust and respect. If you read or listen to most of today's mega-entrepreneurs, they've all used coaches, non-executive directors and mentors to assist them on their journey. It's no different for major sports people, they have a coach. Many have more than one, with specialists to cover diet, fitness, mental and technical aspects.

If you like what I've shared with you here, Better Never Stops is here to enable you to implement the SECCESS® system in your business. We'll take you through the seven steps, guiding and helping you to fall back in love with your business, restoring your mojo and living your dream.

HOW TO STAY IN LOVE WITH YOUR BUSINESS...
THE ENTREPRENEUR'S GUIDE TO HAVING FUN AND LIVING THE DREAM

Of course, Better Never Stops, so we can't just leave it there. Running a business is a continuous process, it doesn't stop changing or evolving. In this book I've shared many times the dangers of standing still and not developing your business. This will only lead you to soon start falling out of love again with your business and all the old painful symptoms will come back into your life.

That's why our seven step SECCESS® System is built on an infinity loop, so once you finish one lap you start the process again building upon the good work you've already implemented. You may ask "Why haven't you given all of them here?" And that would be a fair question. I can assure you I've found it hard not to. But the truth is, there is only so much change you can implement during a period because:

- Time constraints: you must continue to run the business and generate profit without too much disruption.

- Changing too much, too quickly can be very unsettling for people.

- Developing and growing a business is an evolution and not a revolution.

- There's a systematic process that needs to happen in a certain order.

My next book (published in 2020), How To Stay In Love With Your Business, will take you through the seven steps again, with the next evolution of plans and techniques to implement which will ensure you to have even more fun in your business and live the life your dreams desire.

ACKNOWLEDGEMENTS

This feels like an Oscar speech when the winner begins with, "Oh my god, where do I start" and, inevitably, has tear-filled eyes. Those that know me well will have seen me get slightly emotional when thanking those who I owe so much to. I'll try to keep this short and sweet and keep my emotions in check.

However, there are so many people who have helped me along the journey of writing my first book and my life. I'll keep these acknowledgements to mainly my book otherwise we would be here a long time, "I'd like to thank my teacher in primary school…"

I'll start with Lucy, Daniel and the team at Dent who inspired me, and gave me the structure, support and guidance to even think writing my first book was possible, let alone now completed.

For my editors, Suzanne, Auntie Di and Justin Alistair Lowde, who have painstakingly taken my jumbled up dyslexic draft book and turned it into something that makes sense (well it makes sense to me).

My beta readers, Andy Lucas, Simon Biggs, Jason Ford and Peter Richardson for the time they invested and their valuable constructive feedback.

For Slobodan Solaja who created the wonderful design and layout. Oh, and my friends, colleagues and family who voted on the choice of design.

To Richard Jackson MBE, from Mancroft International, who's provided such a wonderful foreword for this book and I look forward to partnering with.

My awesome accountability group, Selina, Tom, Gareth, Jake and Mike, who have supported and encouraged me along the way.

For my clients, particularly Adrian Lewis, Steve Tarrant, Chris Smith and Peter Richardson, who have supported me and allowed me to work with them.

To my amazing family, Haiden, Hannah, Mat and my mum, who inspire, motivate me and make it all worthwhile.

And finally my gorgeous Suzanne, who has put up with me writing at 'silly-o'clock' in the morning. I'm so lucky to have you in my life and by my side xxx.

ABOUT THE AUTHOR

Adrian Peck is an entrepreneur and author. Since 2011 he has been coaching business owners via his Grow Your Business and Better Never Stops brands.

Adrian has always had a keen interest in business and comes from an entrepreneurial family. After the Second World War, his great grandmother Mabel Peck and her second-hand shop were infamous in Ipswich. Adrian's father Alan Peck ran various successful businesses during his life, the most well-known being Star Lines, which he grew from a small corner shop into the largest kitchen and bathroom retailer in Suffolk. Now, his brothers, Roger and Patrick, run a similar business in Ipswich called KBB.

By the age of twenty Adrian had started his first business, repairing cars in a village garage, before being lured to the AA to become a Patrol fixing cars on the roadside.

On the 12th April 1995 something happened that turned his life upside down: his brother Ian was killed in a car accident. In the previous September Ian had celebrated his 30th birthday and was married with two young daughters. Adrian was very close to Ian, only two days previously they'd been together when Adrian cooked a family Sunday roast.

"They say that "out of tragedy comes something good". Apart from the horrific hole his death left in our lives, this day also changed my life in several good ways. My outlook and approach to life certainly changed."

Adrian went back to education to realise he was dyslexic and not thick after all! He took evening classes to learn more about business, obtaining an HNC in Business Studies and another in Management. Following a successful corporate career working with blue-chip UK companies, after 13 years of spending far too much work time on trains, planes and automobiles, hotels, motorways, airports and taxis Adrian decided it was time for a change.

Adrian decided to do something that was quite novel for him, live and work in Suffolk. He wanted to be at home more and to somehow use his extensive knowledge, expertise and disciplines from working in corporate environments. In 2011 he set up his own business to help others get more from their businesses. Since then Adrian has met and helped hundreds of business owners, helping them become more fulfilled and rewarded and less stressed.

Adrian Peck

In 2018 Better Never Stops was born as he developed the business to have a much further reach to enable many more people to achieve great things in their lives.

To find out more about Adrian, go to
www.linkedin.com/in/adrianjpeck/

BIGGER PURPOSE...

"To enable ambitious entrepreneurs to enjoy their journey, live their dream and leave them feeling inspired and empowered to grow sustainable successful businesses that make a positive impact on their local community."

There are thousands of great entrepreneurs out there, running technically sound companies, but they could achieve so much more with the right help and guidance. That's why I've created Better Never Stops. I have a passion for fixing business problems, creating innovative solutions and seeing the results achieved by my clients.

Alone, there's only so much I can achieve and so much impact I can have on the world. At least that's what I believed. I thought you had to be a multi-millionaire like Bill Gates or Richard Branson to make a bigger impact on the world.

B1G1 – Business For Good

That was until I found this amazing organisation, and the awesome work Masami Sato and Paul Dunn are doing. Aligned to the 17 United Nations Sustainable Goals, their platform and the projects they sponsor are transforming lives across the globe. Through it, ordinary people like you and me CAN make a big impact on the world.

Every purchase of this book will provide a day's business training for a young entrepreneur – to see how many business days we've provided so far, go to
www.betterneverstops.global/IMPACT

For out more about B1G1, go to www.b1g1.com

WHAT'S NEXT

1. Connect with me on Linked-in –
   https://www.linkedin.com/in/adrianjpeck/

2. See how fit your business is, take our business health
   check – www.myhealthcheck.biz

3. Review this book on Amazon

4. Go to B1G1 and make an immediate impact to someones
   life…